CAMPAIGN 327

PECKUWE 1780

The Revolutionary War on the Ohio River Frontier

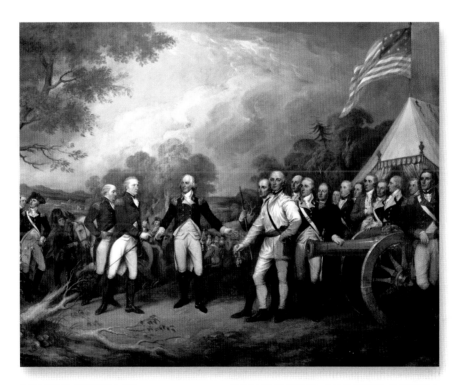

JOHN F. WINKLER

ILLUSTRATED BY PETER DENNIS
Series editor Marcus Cowper

Osprey Publishing
c/o Bloomsbury Publishing Plc
PO Box 883, Oxford, OX1 9PL, UK
Or
c/o Bloomsbury Publishing Inc.
1385 Broadway, 5th Floor, New York, NY 10018, USA
Email: info@ospreypublishing.com

www.ospreypublishing.com

OSPREY is a trademark of Osprey Publishing Ltd, a division of Bloomsbury
Publishing Plc.

First published in Great Britain in 2018

© 2018 Osprey Publishing Ltd

A CIP catalog record for this book is available from the British Library.

ISBN: PB: 978 1 4728 2884 2
          ePub: 978 1 4728 2885 9
          ePDF: 978 1 4728 2886 6
          XML: 978 1 4728 2887 3

18 19 20 21 22   10 9 8 7 6 5 4 3 2 1

Index by Alan Rutter
Typeset in Myriad Pro and Sabon
Maps by Bounford.com
3D BEVs by The Black Spot
Page layouts by PDQ Digital Media Solutions, Bungay, UK
Printed in China through World Print Ltd.

Artist's note

Readers may care to note that the original paintings from which the color
plates in this book were prepared are available for private sale. All
reproduction copyright whatsoever is retained by the Publishers. All
enquiries should be addressed to:

Peter Dennis, Fieldhead, The Park, Mansfield, Notts, NG18 2AT, UK
Email: magie.h@ntlworld.com

The Publishers regret that they can enter into no correspondence upon
this matter.

Osprey Publishing supports the Woodland Trust, the UK's leading woodland
conservation charity. Between 2014 and 2018, our donations are being
spent on their Centenary Woods project in the UK.

To find out more about our authors and books, visit
www.ospreypublishing.com. Here you will find extracts, author
interviews, details of forthcoming events and the option to sign up for
our newsletter.

Author's acknowledgements

Jim Campbell and Bill Smith provided information on details and locations
of battle events, and the weapons used. Terry Brown, Chris Crowley, Carol
Kennard, and Nancy Wallace of the Greene County Park (Ohio) District
offered assistance in exploring the battlefield and nearby area. Dale
Benington and John Stanton supplied illustrations from their vast
collections of 18th-century site photographs. Jeff Dearth and Mel Hankla
provided photographs of surviving weapons, and Lance Greene a
photograph of an artifact his archaeology students unearthed while the
book was being written. Lorie Arendt, Leslie Arendt, Harmony Arendt, Chris
Crowley, and Tom Ratterman supplied pictures of the battlefield. Les
Daugherty and Keith Morrison of the Ruddell and Martin Stations Historical
Association provided photographs of other sites.

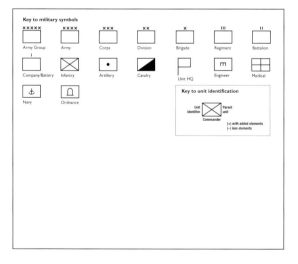

CONTENTS

Eastern North America in 1780.

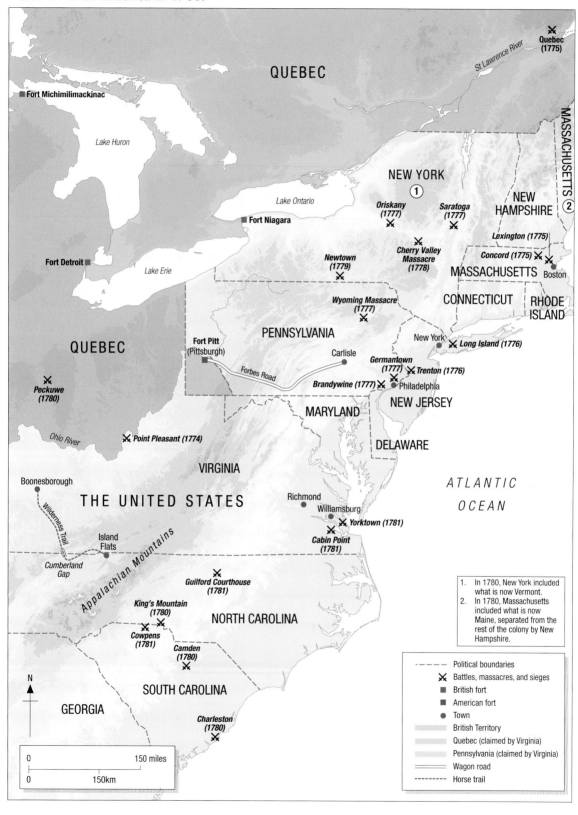

QUEBEC

St Lawrence River

Quebec (1775) ✕

Fort Michimilimackinac ■

Lake Huron

Lake Ontario

Fort Niagara ■

Fort Detroit ■

Lake Erie

MASSACHUSETTS ②

NEW YORK ①

Oriskany (1777) ✕

Saratoga (1777) ✕

NEW HAMPSHIRE

Cherry Valley Massacre (1778) ✕

Lexington (1775) ✕
Concord (1775) ✕
Boston ●

Newtown (1779) ✕

MASSACHUSETTS

CONNECTICUT

Wyoming Massacre (1777) ✕

RHODE ISLAND

QUEBEC

PENNSYLVANIA

Fort Pitt (Pittsburgh) ■

Carlisle

New York ●
Long Island (1776) ✕

Forbes Road

Germantown (1777) ✕
Trenton (1776) ✕

Peckuwe (1780) ✕

Brandywine (1777) ✕
Philadelphia ●

NEW JERSEY

MARYLAND

Ohio River

Point Pleasant (1774) ✕

DELAWARE

VIRGINIA

THE UNITED STATES

Boonesborough

Richmond ●
Williamsburg ●

Yorktown (1781) ✕

Cabin Point (1781) ✕

Appalachian Mountains

Island Flats

Wilderness Trail

Cumberland Gap

ATLANTIC OCEAN

Guilford Courthouse (1781) ✕

King's Mountain (1780) ✕

NORTH CAROLINA

Cowpens (1781) ✕

Camden (1780) ✕

N

SOUTH CAROLINA

GEORGIA

Charleston (1780) ✕

1. In 1780, New York included what is now Vermont.
2. In 1780, Massachusetts included what is now Maine, separated from the rest of the colony by New Hampshire.

– – – –	Political boundaries
✕	Battles, massacres, and sieges
■	British fort
■	American fort
●	Town
	British Territory
	Quebec (claimed by Virginia)
	Pennsylvania (claimed by Virginia)
	Wagon road
- - - - -	Horse trail

0 _____ 150 miles
0 _____ 150km

ORIGINS OF THE CAMPAIGN

THE OHIO RIVER FRONTIER

Five years after the April 19, 1775 battles of Lexington and Concord, the Revolutionary War still continued in 1780. Most of the nearly 2.6 million Americans, hundreds of thousands of whom supported the British, lived within 100 miles of the Atlantic. About 30,000, however, lived far to the west, on the Ohio River frontier.

Four geographical features defined this remote area. Two were water routes upon which boats could transport soldiers and supplies to the frontier from the Atlantic Ocean. The first, controlled by the British, led 800 miles from Quebec up the St Lawrence River, and through Lake Ontario and Lake Erie, to Detroit, the main British stronghold in the West. The second was controlled by the Spanish, who were allied with the Americans in the war. It led 700 miles up the Mississippi River from New Orleans to St Louis, a French settlement that served as the capital of Spanish Upper Louisiana.

The third feature was the Ohio River, which extended 1,000 miles from Pittsburgh to the Mississippi. Northwest of the river was an area claimed by both the British, as part of the province of Quebec, and Virginia. There, more than 5,000 French settlers lived in Detroit, Kaskaskia, Cahokia, and

Although the French had begun settling on the frontier in 1701, defeat in the French and Indian War had forced France to cede its territory east of the Mississippi to Britain, and west of the river to Spain, in 1763. This 1740 French settler's house in Cahokia survives at Cahokia Courthouse State Historic Site. (Courtesy of the Illinois Historic Preservation Agency)

Vincennes, which the Americans called St Vin. About 400 Christian Delaware Indians, converted by the Moravian missionaries David Zeisberger and John Heckewelder, lived as farmers and artisans in Schönbrunn, Gnadenhütten, and other towns.

Those populations, however, were overshadowed by nearly 30,000 other Indians in the area, who lived much as their ancestors had for centuries. Warriors of the Delaware, Kickapoo, Miami, Mingo, Ojibwe, Ottawa, Piankashaw, Potawatomi, Sauk, Shawnee, Wea, Winnebago, Wyandot, and other tribes roamed the woods, hunting or battling enemies, as their women, children, and slaves tended the cornfields at their scattered villages.

The fourth was the Appalachian Mountains, which rose between the Atlantic coast and the Ohio River. This massive barrier, sometimes called the "Endless Mountains," limited the ability of the Americans to fight on the Ohio River frontier. They could dispatch men and supplies to it only with difficulty and at great expense.

Between the Appalachians and the Ohio River were the American frontier settlers. Almost all were on the upper Ohio, where settlement had begun in 1765. Fort Pitt at Pittsburgh, Fort Henry at Wheeling, and forts Armstrong and Crawford to the north, guarded two small urban centers, Pittsburgh and Hannastown, and hundreds of settlers' fortified stations and homesteads.

Two tenuous lines of communication and supply led across the mountains to the upper Ohio. Pennsylvanians followed Forbes Road, a wagon road from Carlisle, PA to Pittsburgh. Only on this 268-mile-long path could anything heavier than a packhorse's 250lb load reach the Ohio frontier. Virginians followed Braddock's Road from near Winchester, VA, which in sections was too steep for wagon traffic.

Both Pennsylvania and Virginia claimed the area around Pittsburgh. Six years before, the Earl of Dunmore, the royal governor of Virginia, had seized it for his colony by force. Now Pennsylvania and Virginia exercised joint control of the area until the dispute could be resolved.

To obtain support for his action from the western settlers, Dunmore had in 1774 provoked a war with the Mingos and Shawnees. He and Colonel Andrew Lewis had then led armies into Ohio. Units of Dunmore's army had defeated the Indians at the August 2, 1774 Battle of Wakatomica and October 27, 1774 Battle of Seekunk. Lewis's army had prevailed at a much larger engagement, the October 10, 1774 Battle of Point Pleasant.

At the site of Point Pleasant, 283 miles down the Ohio from Pittsburgh, lay Fort Randolph. This Virginia militia stronghold at the mouth of the Kanawha River guarded the almost empty middle Ohio River frontier. There, protected by small settlers' fortresses like Prickett's Fort, near what is now Fairmont, West VA, and Fort Donnally, near modern Lewisburg, West VA, a few thousand widely scattered settlers lived on or near the Kanawha, New, Greenbrier, Monongahela and Tygart Valley rivers at the end of horse trails from Maryland and Virginia.

In 1775, Dunmore fled from Williamsburg, the Virginia capital. Patrick Henry, and then Thomas Jefferson, succeeded him as governor. The photograph shows the reconstructed Governor's Palace at Colonial Williamsburg. (Carol M. Highsmith Archive, Library of Congress, Prints and Photographs Division)

Still further down the Ohio was Kentucky, which the Virginia victory at Point Pleasant had opened to settlement. There, a much smaller group of Americans lived in two areas. The first, where settlement had begun in 1775, was in central Kentucky. There, the largest settlements were Harrodsburg, Ruddell's Station, Lexington, Bryan's Station, Boonesborough, and Logan's Station. The second area, where settlement had begun in 1778, was at the Falls of the Ohio, 2-mile-long rapids in which the water fell 26ft. There, 706 miles down the river from Pittsburgh, Fort at the Falls guarded Louisville and many smaller stations and homesteads.

Kentucky could be reached by two routes. The first was from Pittsburgh on the Ohio River. The second was from Virginia on the Wilderness Trail. This path, a horse trail from Island Flats, now Kingsport, TN, led through the Cumberland Gap in the Appalachians.

Crawford, a close friend of George Washington, would lead the 7th Virginia at the September 11, 1777 Battle of Brandywine, the October 4, 1777 Battle of Germantown, and other engagements. This Robert O. Chadeayne portrait of Crawford is displayed at the Wyandot County Museum in Upper Sandusky, Ohio. (Courtesy of the Wyandot County Historical Society, Upper Sandusky, Ohio)

In 1775, James Harrod had led the first Kentucky settlers down the Ohio to Harrodsburg, and Daniel Boone another party along the Wilderness Trail to Boonesborough. Before the year ended, many young veterans of Lord Dunmore's War had joined them. Twenty-five-year-old John Todd, who had fought at Point Pleasant, arrived, as did 21-year-old Samuel Wells, and 20-year-old Simon Kenton, who was known on the frontier as Simon Butler.

The new settlers included 22-year-old George Rogers Clark, who had learned the craft of war as one of Dunmore's company captains. His teachers had been Michael Cresap and Daniel Morgan, older men who also led companies in Colonel William Crawford's regiment. At the outbreak of the Revolutionary War, Cresap, Morgan, and Crawford had crossed the mountains to join Washington's Continental Army. Although Cresap would die of illness a few months later, Morgan and Crawford would distinguish themselves. Clark, however, had not followed them. His future, he had thought, was in Kentucky.

Soon, 25-year-old John Floyd, who had led one of Lewis's companies, 33-year-old Benjamin Logan, and 26-year-old William Whitley, arrived to join the Kentucky settlers. The newcomers brought word of events that had occurred east of the Appalachians months before. An American invasion of Canada had ended in disaster at the December 31, 1775 Battle of Quebec. But on March 17, 1776, the British had left Boston, their last important stronghold in America.

On June 6, 1776, Clark called for a meeting in Harrodsburg to organize the settlements as a Virginia county. On June 15, the settlers chose him and another man as emissaries to travel to Williamsburg. There they were to ask the new revolutionary government of Virginia for gunpowder and recognition of Kentucky as a county.

At the July 20, 1776 Battle of Island Flats, the settlers would defeat the attacking Indians. More than 5,000 American militiamen from four states then would burn the Cherokees' towns and end the war. The photograph shows reconstructed Joseph Martin's Station, at Wilderness Road State Park near Roseville, VA. (Graphic Enterprises)

After passing through the Cumberland Gap, Clark and his companion received a shock. At Joseph Martin's Station, the first settlement beyond the gap, they found no settlers. "We sat still for a few moments looking at each other," Clark remembered, "and I found myself reduced to a state of perfect despair."

When the frightened Kentuckians reached Island Flats, they learned why Joseph Martin's Station had been abandoned. On July 3, 1776, hundreds of Cherokee warriors, led by the great war chief Dragging Canoe, had attacked American settlements in what is now Virginia, North Carolina, South Carolina, and Georgia.

A second shock awaited Clark in Williamsburg. Like most Americans, he had thought the war would end in compromise. The 13 Colonies had formed a temporary alliance to conduct the war, and sent delegates to the Continental Congress in Philadelphia to coordinate their actions. But when the war was over, and the Americans had won the rights they had demanded, they would remain British. Instead, the astonished Clark learned, the Continental Congress had on July 4 announced that the colonies would together form an independent nation, the United States of America.

On August 23, the new Virginia government provided 500lb of gunpowder, and also promised to create Kentucky County. But before Clark left Williamsburg, ominous news arrived. The British had returned to America in overwhelming force. At the August 27 Battle of Long Island, Washington's army had barely escaped annihilation. On September 15, the British had occupied New York.

Eager for adventure, Clark's 21-year-old first cousin Joseph Rogers, and seven other young men volunteered to travel back to Kentucky with Clark. But as they went down the Ohio River, fire came from the banks. Excited by the Cherokee attacks, the Mingo chief Pluggy and Shawnee Black Fish had decided to resume Lord Dunmore's War. Now their warriors were attacking the new settlements in Kentucky. Pursued by Indians, Clark's party reached Harrodsburg safely. But the situation in Kentucky, he was told, was desperate. Most of the settlers who had arrived in 1776 had fled back to Virginia. Only 250 remained.

On Christmas Day, Mingo warriors attacked a party of settlers led by Todd, capturing Rogers and three others. On December 29, they assaulted recently established McLelland's Station. Pluggy fell in the attack, but the Kentucky settlers decided to abandon all but the three strongest fortresses: Harrodsburg, Boonesborough, and Logan's Station.

In the spring of 1777, more new settlers arrived. They included Indian fighters like Edward Bulger, who were sorely needed. Again and again, Black Fish's warriors came from Chalawgatha, a Shawnee town on the Little Miami

The Ohio River frontier.

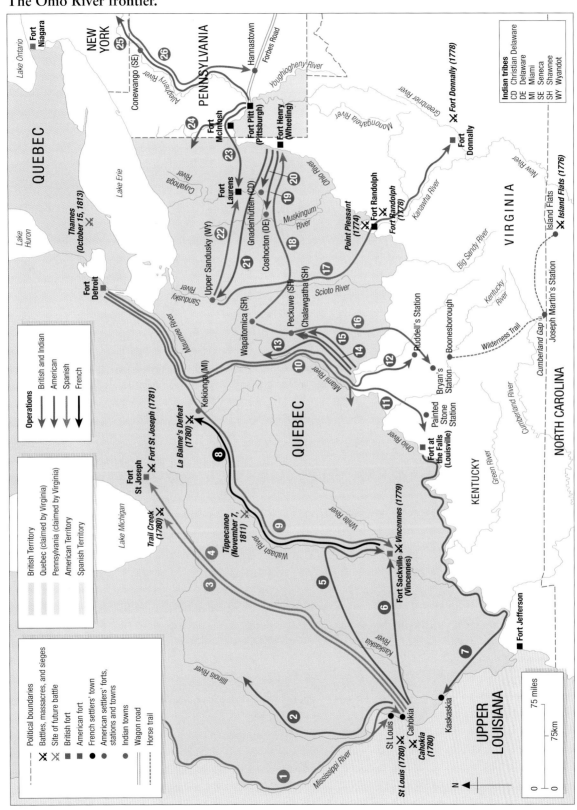

River. On March 7, they struck Harrodsburg and Boonesborough. On April 24, they again assailed Boonesborough, where Kenton saved a wounded Boone from death. On May 23, they attacked Boonesborough yet again. They then besieged Logan's Station from May 27 until June 1.

Soon it would grow worse. George Germain, Viscount Sackville, the British Secretary of State for the American Department, directed British operations to suppress the rebellion. For two years, he had not encouraged the Indians to attack the Americans, but now he finally ordered his commanders to recruit Indian allies. First they sought aid from the powerful Iroquois, a confederacy of the Mohawk, Oneida, Onondaga, Cayuga, Seneca, and Tuscorora tribes in upstate New York. All but the Oneida agreed to fight with the British.

Lieutenant-Governor Henry Hamilton, who directed British operations in the West, then convened in Detroit a council of Ohio Indians. Led by the great chief White Eyes, the Delawares refused to join the British. Cornstalk, who had led the Shawnees at Point Pleasant, declined any command. The Thawakila, one of the five Shawnee subgroups, emigrated to Missouri to avoid the war.

But the Chalawgatha, Kispoko, Mequachake, and Peckuwe Shawnees agreed to fight. Led by the great war chief Blue Jacket, they joined Black Fish's warriors. Half King and Tarhe's Wyandots, Egushwa's Ottawas, and Little Turtle's Miamis also became British allies.

By September, Hamilton reported, 1,150 warriors were searching the Ohio River frontier for Americans to kill or capture. On September 1, Half King and 200 warriors attacked Fort Henry. On September 26, they ambushed Captain James Foreman and 44 militiamen at McMechen's Narrows, killing Foreman and 22 others.

As Fall approached, a quarter of the remaining Kentucky settlers announced that they were leaving their three strongholds for Virginia. To the surprise of many, Clark offered to lead them back across the mountains. When they departed on October 1, only 65 men remained to defend Harrodsburg, 22 at Boonesborough, and 15 at Logan's Station.

The September 1, 1777, attack on Fort Henry would be remembered for "McColloch's Leap." While leading a 40-man relief force, Major Samuel McColloch was cut off by the Wyandots. To their astonishment, he escaped unharmed by riding his horse more than 200ft down this wooded cliff from the exposed area in the upper center. (Dale Benington)

AN AMERICA BEYOND THE APPALACHIANS

Clark had accompanied the settlers for a reason of his own. When not fighting Black Fish's Indians, he later wrote, his time had been "devoted to reflecting upon things in general, particularly whether or not it accorded with the interests of the United States to support Kentucky." In Williamsburg, he asked a surprised Patrick Henry and Thomas Jefferson to persuade the Virginia government to approve a secret mission. He made his proposal at the right time.

After Clark's first trip to Williamsburg, Washington had restored American confidence by defeating the British at Trenton on December 26, 1776. But in 1777, two British armies had advanced. Major-General Sir William Howe's force had defeated the Americans at Brandywine and Germantown, and occupied Philadelphia. Lieutenant-General Sir John Burgoyne's army, however, had marched to disaster. After defeat at the October 7, 1777 Battle of Saratoga, the British commander had been forced to surrender his 7,000 men. That, the exultant Virginians thought, had assured American independence.

On January 2, 1778, a delighted Clark learned that his mission had been approved. Commissioned a Virginia militia lieutenant-colonel, he was to recruit a regiment of Upper Ohio frontiersmen, and lead them down the Ohio to an undisclosed destination. Two days later, Clark left for Pittsburgh.

As Clark rode up Braddock's Road, Brigadier-General Edward Hand, the senior American commander on the Upper Ohio, was assembling an army of 500 militiamen to attack a British supply base at the mouth of the Cuyahoga River. Led by the adopted Mingo Simon Girty, who had guided Dunmore's army into Ohio in 1774, they left Pittsburgh on February 1. When a snowstorm forced Hand to halt near the present Ohio border, some of his militiamen followed tracks to a nearby Indian camp. Unable to distinguish hostile Wyandots from neutral Delawares, they there killed the mother, father, and sons of the prominent Delaware chief Captain Pipe.

When Clark reached Pittsburgh on February 10, he began recruiting. Devastating news then arrived from Kentucky. On an expedition to get

Daniel Morgan's 500-man Rifle Corps played a critical role in the American victory at Saratoga. John Trumbull's "Surrender of General Burgoyne," which hangs in the rotunda of the US Capitol, depicts Morgan, the imposing figure in white to the right of center. (Author's collection)

By 1778, a small population of black slaves lived on the frontier. Several, like Big Sam at Fort Henry, Monk Estill at Estill's Station in Kentucky, and Dick Pointer at Fort Donnally, won fame as defenders of the settlements. When Half King's Wyandots attacked Fort Donnally on May 29, Pointer saved the 60 settlers by repelling the Indians' initial assault with this musket. (Courtesy of the West Virginia State Museum)

From this ridge overlooking Kaskaskia, Clark's men first saw the Mississippi River, which would be the western boundary of the United States until 1803. In 1777, the Mississippi flowed beyond the forested area ahead, now separated from the ridge by the river's modern course. (John Stanton)

salt for the settlements, Boone and 26 others had been captured by Black Fish's Shawnees on February 8. There was also bad news on the upper Ohio. He found few men willing to enlist for his secret mission. Pennsylvanians refused to join a Virginia unit. And there were many loyalists. Unhappy at his treatment by Hand and other officers, Girty fled Pittsburgh to join the British on March 27. With him went Alexander McKee, who had been the chief British Indian agent in Pittsburgh, and Matthew Elliott, a prominent trader. The three soon would provide invaluable aid to the British cause.

After three months, Clark was finally able to assemble about 200 men, who assumed that their mission would be to aid the Kentucky settlers. On May 12, Clark led them down the Ohio. Four days later, Half King and 200 Wyandots began a siege of Fort Randolph. By May 22, when Clark's regiment reached the fort, the Indians had departed. They had moved up the Kanawha River to attack weaker Fort Donnally.

When their boats passed the mouth of the Kentucky River, the water route to the Kentucky settlements, Clark's men were puzzled. On May 27, they halted at the Falls of the Ohio. Their 24-year-old commander then revealed at last the mission they would undertake.

In Williamsburg, Clark had posed a question that no one had considered. If the United States was to be an independent country, what was to be its western boundary? It should be, Clark had argued, the western border claimed by Virginia: the Great Lakes and the Mississippi River. To secure a border on the Great Lakes, the Americans must capture Detroit. Henry and Jefferson, he explained, were persuading Congress to detach from Washington's army a force to take the British fortress. To secure a border on the Mississippi, the Americans must capture Kaskaskia, Cahokia, and Vincennes. They, he told his listeners, were the officers and men of the Illinois Regiment, which had been formed to undertake that mission. After building a fort at the Falls, they would go down the Ohio, seize the towns, and establish an American border opposite the Spanish on the Mississippi.

Clark, thought many in his stunned audience, was mad. A force that should be used to protect the beleaguered Kentucky settlements was instead to be wasted on a pointless and perilous adventure. Many of his soldiers began deserting.

Todd, Kenton, and several other Kentuckians, however, arrived to join Clark's force. On June 24, they went down the Ohio. Ten days later, they celebrated the first anniversary of the 4th of July by capturing Kaskaskia. On July 7, they took Cahokia. On July 20, Kenton led a party of Clark's men to Vincennes, where they captured British Fort Sackville.

Without losing a man, Clark had fulfilled his mission. Henry and Jefferson, moreover, had accomplished theirs. On February 6, France had recognized the United States as an independent country. Facing war with this formidable new enemy, the British had decided to abandon Philadelphia and concentrate their forces in New York. On June 1, a jubilant Congress had approved a campaign against Detroit. Washington had ordered Brigadier-General Lachlan McIntosh to lead 500 Continental Army regulars to Pittsburgh, where he would replace Hand. Joined by Pennsylvania and Virginia militiamen, he then would march against the British stronghold.

As McIntosh moved west on Forbes Road, Todd began organizing the captured territory as Illinois County, Virginia. Clark assumed responsibility for diplomatic approaches to America's new western neighbors. First he charmed the French and Spanish in St Louis. The Kentuckian's "wisdom and affability," Spanish Lieutenant-Governor Francisco de Leyba wrote to Patrick Henry, "have made him generally loved by all who know him." Francis Vigo, a prominent merchant, pledged his resources to the American cause. And Clark was himself charmed in St Louis. Her name was Teresa, and they planned to marry after the war.

McIntosh was a Georgia political figure with little military experience. This Henry Hoppner Meyer engraving reproduced a James P. Longacre portrait of McIntosh. (Library of Congress, Prints and Photographs Division)

The Kentuckian then addressed the western Indians, whose neutrality he was eager to preserve. At a council in Cahokia, Clark became a legend. First he astonished the Winnebagos. After learning of a plot to assassinate him, he had the guilty chiefs brought to the council in chains. Two young Winnebago warriors, their heads covered by blankets, then knelt before him and asked that he take their lives instead of those of their chiefs. Clark rose, removed the blankets, extended his hand, and raised the men to their feet. Whether the Winnebagos decided to fight the Americans, or to remain at peace, he shouted, brave men like these should lead them, not skulking assassins.

Clark then noticed the scowling Sauk chief Big Gate. He hoped, the Kentuckian told Big Gate, that the two soon would meet in battle. But since they were still at peace, he continued, he would consider it an honor to eat and drink with such a great warrior. That night, Clark remembered, Big Gate proved to be "a merry fellow."

When word of Clark's achievements crossed the mountains, emigration to Kentucky resumed again. And in the West, White Eyes concluded that the Americans were going to win the war. His people, the visionary chief thought, must learn to live like the Christian Delaware. They then could become the nucleus of a confederacy of Ohio Indians, which could in time form a new state in the American union. Using his great prestige, he persuaded his people to enter the war as American allies and to fight with McIntosh.

On August 10, McIntosh arrived at Pittsburgh with Colonel John Gibson's 13th Virginia Regiment and Colonel Daniel Brodhead's 8th Pennsylvania. Gibson, an adopted Delaware, had led a company in Dunmore's army, and translated in 1774 the famous speech of the Mingo chief Logan. After leading the 6th Virginia Regiment at Trenton, Brandywine, Germantown, and other battles, he had assumed command of the 13th Virginia. Brodhead, a miller and farmer before the war, was recognized for special bravery at Long Island. After promotion, he led the 8th Pennsylvania at Trenton, Brandywine, and Germantown.

On August 13, Boone, who had escaped from Chalawgatha, returned to Kentucky. Colonel John Bowman, who had assumed command of the Kentucky militia, was eager to attack the town. He dispatched Kenton and two other frontiersmen to scout Chalawgatha for an operation against it. As they were crossing the Ohio on September 7, Black Fish and 450 Indians surrounded Boonesborough. Led by Boone, the 40 defenders survived a ten-day siege. But when Black Fish returned to Chalawgatha, there was consolation. Kenton had been captured on September 13.

In Detroit, Hamilton had in 1777 welcomed warriors bringing 129 scalps and 72 prisoners. By October 1, 1778, he had received another 210 scalps and 55 captives. But Clark's successes, and the prospect of McIntosh's campaign, had alarmed the Indians. The worried British commander summoned Captain Henry Bird with reinforcements from Fort Niagara.

Hamilton then received good news. After reconsidering the likely cost of capturing Detroit, Congress had ordered McIntosh to limit his operation to destroying the Wyandot villages on the Sandusky River. Hamilton concluded that he could use his reinforcements for an offensive operation. He first would recapture Vincennes. He would then recover Cahokia and Kaskaskia, and destroy the American fort at the Falls of the Ohio.

The 1778 siege of Fort Boonesborough would be remembered for the ingenuity of the combatants. Squire Boone, who would lead a company at Peckuwe, crafted fire extinguishers from musket barrels and waterproof bags. Others bored a tree trunk to create a wooden 6lb gun, which cracked after one firing. When the Indians tried to tunnel under the stockade wall, the defenders ended the attempt by digging a countermine. These re-enactors at reconstructed Fort Boonesborough are celebrating the end of the siege. (Graphic Enterprises)

On October 13, McIntosh left Fort Pitt with the largest army assembled in the West during the war. Fifteen hundred American regulars and militiamen marched to meet White Eyes' Delawares on the Tuscarawas River. On November 19, they began to build Fort Laurens, a fortress that would serve as a base for operations in Ohio. But the following day, word spread that White Eyes was dead. Smallpox had claimed the great chief, it was reported, though some said an American militiaman had killed him.

On November 29, Fort Laurens was completed. But instead of advancing to the Sandusky River, McIntosh announced that his army would return to Fort Pitt. On December 9, he marched back to Pittsburgh, leaving Gibson and 150 unhappy men to garrison the isolated stronghold, and Killbuck, White Eyes' successor, to retain for the Americans the loyalty of the Delawares.

VINCENNES

Two days before McIntosh's departure, Hamilton had arrived at Vincennes with 400 British soldiers and Indian warriors, and artillery. When he demanded the surrender of Fort Sackville, the small American garrison complied. Hamilton then awaited Indian reinforcements for a further advance to Cahokia.

On January 29, 1779, Vigo, who had been in Vincennes on business, reached Clark, who was in Kaskaskia, with news of Vincennes' fall. Clark could muster few men, and had no artillery, but he nonetheless decided to attack. "I know the case is desperate," he wrote to Patrick Henry on February 3, "but great things have been effected by a few men well conducted."

Two days later, Clark's available Illinois Regiment soldiers, and two companies of Kaskaskia and Cahokia militiamen, marched toward Vincennes through ground flooded by melting snows. For 12 days, his 170 men went forward through mud up to their knees. Then, with their food almost exhausted, they reached the swollen Embarrass River. Through 5 miles of ice-filled water, Clark and his men swam from one island of high ground to the next beside small rafts carrying their supplies.

On February 23, Clark's starving, soaked, and freezing men reached Vincennes. To conceal the size of his force, Clark commenced his attack at night. By the morning of the 24th, his men were concealed in an entrenchment encircling Fort Sackville at a distance of 200 yards. When the American commander boldly demanded surrender, Hamilton refused.

Clark then heard the sound of whooping. Fourteen Indians and Canadian militiamen were returning to Vincennes from Kentucky with scalps and two captives. Clark sent a party to rescue the prisoners. After killing eight of the Indians and Canadians, Clark's men brought to him the freed Kentuckians and six surviving raiders. "I had now," Clark later wrote, "a fair opportunity of making an impression."

The Kentucky commander led the captured raiders to a position ahead of the fort's gate, and ordered the six men to kneel. These men, he shouted to the watching British officers, were not warriors or soldiers. They were vicious killers of women and children.

Clark, remembered Canadian militia Lieutenant Jacob Schieffelin, then approached the kneeling men with a raised tomahawk. The first was an Indian. The man, pled the captain of the Cahokia company, had once saved his life. The second was a Canadian militiaman. He was, begged the company's lieutenant, his only son.

Clark spared the two. But blood from the next four soon covered the ground. The American commander, Schieffelin remembered, dipped his hands into the blood, "rubbing it several times on his cheeks, yelping as a savage." Hamilton, Clark then shouted, must come out to learn the terms of his surrender.

The British commander had good reason to fear his fate if the fort fell. In 1777, the adopted Delaware trader John Leeth had watched him greet a party of warriors arriving in Detroit with prisoners. The Indians, Leeth remembered, displayed "eighteen women and children, poor creatures, dreadfully mangled and emaciated, with their clothes tattered and torn to pieces, in such manner as not to hide their nakedness." He recalled, "If I had had an opportunity, and been supported with strength, I should certainly have killed the governor, who seemed to take great delight in the exhibition."

The fort's gate opened, and Hamilton emerged. Clark, he remembered, "washed his hands and face, still reeking from the human sacrifice in which he had acted as high priest." The Kentuckian then told the British commander that he and his men would be imprisoned in Virginia. At 10.00am on February 25, Clark's army occupied Fort Sackville.

But Hamilton's fort was not the only stronghold under attack. As Clark had marched to Vincennes, Bird, Girty, Half King, and 180 men had surrounded Fort Laurens. On the day Clark had reached Vincennes, the Indians had killed 18 Americans who had ventured beyond its walls. The Americans in the fort, Bird then had announced, must either surrender or starve.

After the war, Hamilton would become governor of Bermuda, where the capital is named for him. The photograph shows the signature page of Thomas Jefferson's copy of the Vincennes articles of capitulation signed by Clark and Hamilton. (Library of Congress, Manuscripts Division)

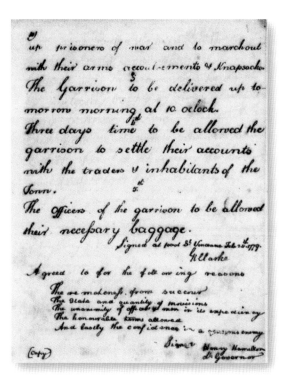

16

The Upper Ohio River frontier.

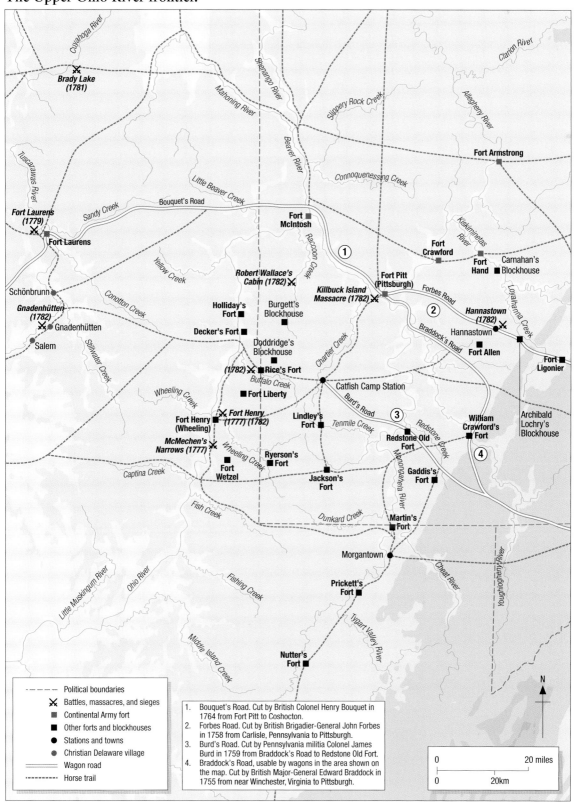

Cuyahoga River

Clarion River

Brady Lake (1781)

Mahoning River

Shenango River

Slippery Rock Creek

Allegheny River

Fort Armstrong

Tuscarawas River

Connoquenessing Creek

Little Beaver Creek

Beaver River

Bouquet's Road

Kiskiminetas River

Sandy Creek

Fort Laurens (1779)

Fort McIntosh

Fort Laurens

Yellow Creek

Raccoon Creek

①

Fort Crawford

Fort Hand

Carnahan's Blockhouse

Robert Wallace's Cabin (1782)

Schönbrunn

Conotton Creek

Killbuck Island Massacre (1782)

Fort Pitt (Pittsburgh)

Forbes Road

Loyalhanna Creek

Gnadenhütten (1782)

Holliday's Fort

Burgett's Blockhouse

②

Hannastown (1782)

Gnadenhütten

Decker's Fort

Chartier Creek

Braddock's Road

Hannastown

Salem

Stillwater Creek

Doddridge's Blockhouse

Fort Allen

Fort Ligonier

(1782) ✕ Rice's Fort

Buffalo Creek

Wheeling Creek

Fort Liberty

Catfish Camp Station

Burd's Road

Fort Henry (1777) (1782)

Lindley's Fort

Tenmile Creek

③

William Crawford's Fort

Archibald Lochry's Blockhouse

McMechen's Narrows (1777)

Wheeling Creek

Ryerson's Fort

Redstone Old Fort

Redstone Creek

④

Fort Wetzel

Jackson's Fort

Gaddis's Fort

Captina Creek

Monongahela River

Little Muskingum River

Fish Creek

Dunkard Creek

Martin's Fort

Ohio River

Fishing Creek

Morgantown

Cheat River

Youghiogheny River

Prickett's Fort

Tygart Valley River

Middle Island Creek

Nutter's Fort

N

---·--- Political boundaries
✕ Battles, massacres, and sieges
■ Continental Army fort
■ Other forts and blockhouses
● Stations and towns
● Christian Delaware village
═══ Wagon road
----- Horse trail

1. Bouquet's Road. Cut by British Colonel Henry Bouquet in 1764 from Fort Pitt to Coshocton.
2. Forbes Road. Cut by British Brigadier-General John Forbes in 1758 from Carlisle, Pennsylvania to Pittsburgh.
3. Burd's Road. Cut by Pennsylvania militia Colonel James Burd in 1759 from Braddock's Road to Redstone Old Fort.
4. Braddock's Road, usable by wagons in the area shown on the map. Cut by British Major-General Edward Braddock in 1755 from near Winchester, Virginia to Pittsburgh.

0   20 miles
0   20km

Gibson responded with bravado, rolling two barrels of pork and flour out of the gate as a gift to the besiegers. But by March 19, his men were eating roots, dried hides, and even their own moccasins. That day, the besiegers fled when a 500-man relief column at last arrived.

CHALAWGATHA

By then, the ineffective McIntosh had been recalled. Brodhead, who succeeded him as American commander on the upper Ohio, was eager to reassure the wavering Delaware. He would, he planned, conduct the following summer the campaign against the Wyandots that his predecessor had abandoned.

Respite from Wyandot raiding was desperately needed. Soon after the relief of Fort Laurens, three Wyandot raiders attacked a cabin filled with women and children near what is now Mt Morris, PA. Forty-four-year-old Experience Bozarth saved them by killing all three Indians with an axe. A few weeks later, other raiders killed Mrs Frederick Heinrich at a cabin near present Greensburg, PA. But pursuing militiamen overtook the raiders, captured one, and rescued Mrs Heinrich's two daughters. Their leader then granted an unusual request. She wanted, 9-year-old Alexandra Heinrich told him, to avenge her mother by killing the captured Indian herself.

Crawford, who had returned to the frontier in 1777, was leading Virginia militiamen in pursuits of the raiders. The famous frontiersman James Smith was equally active in leading Pennsylvania militiamen. But the pursuers of Mrs Heinrich's killers had a new leader, Captain Samuel Brady. Detached from command of his 8th Pennsylvania Regiment company, he soon would lead a formidable band. Dressed as Indians, and aided by Brady's Delaware friend Nanowland, Brady's Rangers would become the most effective American unit in the western war.

Encouraged by Clark's triumph at Vincennes, a small flood of new settlers arrived in Kentucky. They included several capable Indian fighters. Among them were 24-year-old George Bedinger; 26-year-old William Oldham, who had fought with Morgan at Saratoga, and 18-year-old Bland Ballard.

The site of Chalawgatha today, as seen from Oldtown, Ohio. (Public domain)

In central Kentucky, Robert Patterson founded Lexington; William Bryan and his three brothers Bryan's Station; and John Grant, John Martin, and Isaac Ruddell new stations to the northeast. Daniel and Squire Boone left Boonesborough to build Boone's Station and Painted Stone Station. Harrodsburg settlers left for James McAfee's, William McAfee's, and Hugh McGary's new stations. And many from Logan's Station went to John Bowman's and William Whitley's new settlements.

Six hundred new settlers came down the Ohio to the area near the Falls. Another 100 men, led by James Harrod's brother William, arrived to look for good settlement sites, to which they would return in 1780. Among the newcomers Clark found an old friend, William Linn, who had led another company in Crawford's regiment during Lord Dunmore's War. Soon the woods near the Falls resounded with falling trees, which were used to build cabins at the new town of Louisville, and at Linn's, John Floyd's, and Peter Sturgis's nearby stations.

Hamilton had marched to Vincennes with most of the Detroit garrison, leaving the British stronghold vulnerable. With 500 men, Clark believed, he could by a rapid advance from Vincennes take Detroit while it was still lightly defended. The Cahokia settler Daniel de Linctot raised a force of 100 horsemen for the campaign. And Bowman agreed to send 300 Kentuckians.

Linctot's horsemen arrived at Vincennes after a daring raid up the Wabash. But when McGary appeared with 30 men, Clark learned that no other Kentuckians were coming. They had gone with Bowman, McGary told a furious Clark, to attack Chalawgatha.

Few Kentuckians, Bowman had found, were willing to march to Detroit. But when he had proposed to lead them instead against Black Fish's Town, 170 had volunteered. William Harrod's men then had agreed to join them.

The Indians at Chalawgatha, who had conducted countless raids into Kentucky without any response, no longer feared a retaliatory attack. Guided by Whitley, Bowman's 270 men were able to reach the town undetected. In darkness on May 31, they took up positions around Chalawgatha for a dawn assault. But before the attack, a Shawnee warrior discovered them.

In the chaos that followed, Black Fish was mortally wounded. Many of the Shawnees fled to Chalawgatha's large council house. Expecting the other Kentuckians to join them, Bedinger, Oldham, Ballard, and 11 others took up positions facing the wooden structure. But Bowman lost control of his army. The rest of his men scattered to search the town for plunder and horses.

For three hours, the 14 Kentuckians battled the Indians in the council house alone. When all but Bedinger, Oldham, Ballard, and another man were dead, they finally retreated. They found the rest of Bowman's men in panic. Girty was coming with a huge army, someone had said.

Bedinger and Oldham, who assumed command, organized the Kentuckians into a battle line, and then into columns to retreat. After 5 miles, nearly 100 pursuing Indians overtook them. On a hill just beyond Glady Run, they formed a hollow square with more than 200 captured horses in the middle. For nine hours, they exchanged fire with the Indians,

At Glady Run, Edward Bulger introduced an important innovation in frontier warfare. He persuaded Henry Hall and three others to join him in using the captured horses to ride through the Indians, and fire on them from behind. "This new mode of carrying on operations," Hall remembered, "placed the Indians, instead of the whites, as heretofore, on the defensive." Its popularity grew quickly. About 30 Kentuckians fought mounted at Peckuwe. A hundred and fifty would ride in Clark's 1782 campaign. This high ground overlooking Glady Run probably was the birthplace of the Kentucky mounted rifleman, whose units and tactics would play a critical role in frontier combat after the Revolutionary War. (Author's photograph)

who withdrew when darkness fell. The Kentuckians, who had lost ten dead and another ten wounded, then retreated back across the Ohio River.

As Clark raged in Vincennes in furious frustration, Brodhead also fumed. Instead of marching to Fort Laurens and on to the Sandusky River, he had received new orders to march up the Allegheny River to New York.

Aided by Butler's Rangers, a loyalist regiment led by Lieutenant-Colonel John Butler, the Iroquois had had spectacular successes in upstate New York. At the August 6, 1777 Battle of Oriskany, they had ambushed 700 New York militiamen and allied Oneida Iroquois, killing almost 400. At the July 3, 1778 Battle of Wyoming, they had attacked a force of 360 Connecticut militiamen, killing 350 and capturing the rest. At the November 11, 1778 Cherry Valley Massacre, they had killed 44 New York settlers and taken another 45.

Now Brodhead was to join Brigadier-General John Sullivan, who was leading 3,000 American regulars against them. To the despair of Killbuck, the American commander abandoned Fort Laurens on August 2. Nine days later, he led his 600 men north. Although they failed to join Sullivan's army, they destroyed Conewango and ten other undefended Seneca villages.

Soon after Clark returned from Vincennes, he saw in Louisville a man he'd thought dead. After his capture, Kenton had received beatings beyond number. He'd run seven gauntlets. He'd been tied to the stake for burning in Chalawgatha, in Wapatomica, and then in Upper Sandusky. But with the help of Girty and the famous Mingo chief Logan, he had survived and escaped.

Colonel David Rogers and 50 men then appeared on keelboats carrying munitions from New Orleans to Pittsburgh. Clark detached Lieutenant Abraham Chaplin and 23 Illinois Regiment men to reinforce Rogers' force as it went up the Ohio. On October 4, 130 Indians ambushed Rogers' party at the Battle of the Licking River. Girty and Elliott then returned to Chalawgatha with the scalps of Rogers and 44 others, and Chaplin and four other prisoners.

For three years, the Indians had attacked from Chalawgatha. They had failed to drive the Americans from Boonesborough and their other fortresses in Kentucky. But of those who had lived at Boonesborough, where the population had never exceeded 100, the Indians had killed 21 and taken 32 more.

While Chalawgatha stood, the American presence in Kentucky would remain precarious, and Bowman's feeble assault on the Indian base had brought embarrassment instead of relief. The town, the Kentucky settlers agreed, must be destroyed – and they knew who they wanted to lead them against it.

Led by the famous Mohawk chief Joseph Brant, and the Seneca commanders Cornplanter and Big Tree, the Iroquois and Butler's Rangers met Sullivan's army at the August 29, 1779 Battle of Newtown. Sullivan's victory ended large-scale raiding in upstate New York. This tomahawk belonged to Cornplanter. (Jeff Dearth Collection)

CHRONOLOGY

1775

April 19 — Battles of Lexington and Concord.

1776

July 4 — Declaration of Independence.

August 27 — Battle of Long Island.

1777

September 1 — First Attack on Fort Henry.

October 7 — Battle of Saratoga.

1778

May 16–18 — Siege of Fort Randolph.

July 4 — Clark captures Kaskaskia.

September 7–17 — Siege of Fort Boonesborough.

December 17 — British capture Vincennes.

1779

February 22–March 20 — Siege of Fort Laurens.

February 25 — Clark recaptures Vincennes.

June 1 — Battles of Chalawgatha and Glady Run.

August 29 — Battle of Newtown.

October 4 — Battle of Licking River.

1780

May 26 — Battle of St Louis.

June 24 — Surrender of Ruddell's Station.

August 1–14 — Clark's first Ohio campaign.

August 8 — Battle of Peckuwe.

August 16 — Battle of Camden.

October 7 — Battle of King's Mountain.

November 15 — De La Balme's defeat.

1781

January 3 — Battle of Cabin Point.

January 17 — Battle of Cowpens.

February 12 — Spanish capture Fort Joseph.

March 15 — Battle of Guilford Courthouse.

April 20 — Battle of Coshocton.

August 4 — Lochry's defeat.

September 13 — Long Run Massacre.

September 14 — Floyd's defeat.

October 11 — Battle of Brady Lake.

October 19 — Cornwallis surrenders at Yorktown.

1782

March 8 — Gnadenhütten Massacre.

June 4–5 — Battle of Sandusky.

June 6 — Battle of Olentangy.

July 13 — Attack on Hannastown.

August 15–16 — Siege of Bryan's Station.

August 19 — Battle of Blue Licks.

September 11–13 — Second attack on Fort Henry.

November 2–15 — Clark's second Ohio campaign.

November 30 — Treaty of Paris.

OPPOSING COMMANDERS

AMERICAN

The American commander was 27-year-old **Colonel George Rogers Clark**. His principal subordinates led his company of scouts, his Illinois Regiment, and his four Kentucky militia regiments. **Captain Simon Kenton** commanded the company of scouts, usually called spies on the frontier.

Major George Slaughter led the Illinois Regiment. He had served in the Continental Army as major of the 12th Virginia Regiment. His principal subordinates were **Lieutenant Richard Harrison**, who commanded a two-gun artillery company, and captains **Benjamin Roberts** and **Abraham Chaplin**, who led infantry companies. Three months before the battle, Chaplin had escaped from Indian captivity to warn the Kentucky settlers of Bird's invasion.

Lieutenant-colonels **John Floyd**, **William Linn**, **James Harrod**, and **Benjamin Logan** commanded Clark's four militia regiments. Floyd, aged 30 in 1780, had led a company in Andrew Lewis's army during Lord Dunmore's War. His company commanders included captains **Robert Johnson** and **Charles Polk**. Johnson's son Richard Mentor Johnson would win fame at the October 5, 1813 Battle of the Thames, and be elected Vice President of the United States. Polk's senior subordinate was **Lieutenant Samuel Wells**. Brother of the famous adopted Miami William Wells, who was 9 in 1780, Samuel Wells would be the senior Kentucky commander to survive the November 4, 1791 American disaster at Wabash. He later would play an important role at the November 7, 1811 Battle of Tippecanoe, and command the 17th US Infantry Regiment during the War of 1812.

Linn's principal subordinate was **Major Edward Bulger**. Bulger, who had distinguished himself at Glady Run, would fall at the August 19, 1782 Battle of Blue Licks. His company commanders included captains **Lewis Hickman** and **William Oldham**. Hickman, a famous frontiersman, was captured at Peckuwe and later killed. After service in Morgan's Rifle Corps, Oldham had led a company in the 5th Pennsylvania Regiment. He would fall commanding the Kentucky militiamen who fought at Wabash.

At Peckuwe, Oldham was detached from his company to lead the army's advance guard. His senior subordinate was 19-year-old **Lieutenant Bland Ballard**, who had been detached from Roberts's Illinois Regiment company. After the war, Ballard would become one of the most famous Indian fighters on the Ohio River frontier.

James Harrod's company commanders included captains **Squire Boone**, **William Harrod**, **William McAfee**, and **Hugh McGary**. Squire Boone was Daniel Boone's brother. William Harrod, James Harrod's brother, had led a company at Chalawgatha and Glady Run. McAfee would be mortally wounded at Peckuwe. His nephew **Robert B. McAfee** would distinguish himself at Thames and be elected Lieutenant-Governor of Kentucky. McGary, whose rashness would cause a minor defeat during the Peckuwe campaign, would later lead the Kentuckians to disaster at Blue Licks. He would then during Logan's 1786 Ohio campaign murder the friendly Shawnee chief Moluntha, and wound his wife, the famous female chief Nonhelema.

Benjamin Logan, 38 in 1780, served as Clark's second in command. After convening the first Kentucky constitutional convention in 1783, he would lead his own campaign against the Shawnees in 1786, and twice be defeated as a candidate for Kentucky governor. His company commanders included captains **John Logan**, **Robert Patterson**, and **William Whitley**. John Logan was Benjamin Logan's brother. Patterson, who had founded Lexington, would later become one of the leading citizens of Dayton, Ohio, where his 1816 house survives as a museum. Whitley, a legendary frontiersman, was 31 in 1780. At 64, he would return from retirement to fight at Thames, where he would be killed by Tecumseh.

INDIAN

The principal Indian commander was the great chief **Black Hoof** (**Catecahassa**). Aged about 40 in 1780, he had fought in many battles, including Point Pleasant, Chalawgatha, and Glady Run. He would fight at Wabash and the August 20, 1794 Battle of Fallen Timbers, but would then oppose further war with the Americans. In 1813, he would lead the Shawnee at Thames, where they fought as American allies.

Black Fish, a son of the Black Fish who had fallen in 1779, commanded the Chalawgatha Shawnee. He would play a significant role at Wabash. **Wryneck** (**Aquilsika**) led the Peckuwe. **Black Snake** (**Shemeneto**) commanded the Kispoko. **Silver Heels** (**Halowas**), a brother of the great Shawnee commander Cornstalk, led the Mequachake.

The great chief **Buckongahelas**, about 60 in 1780, led the Delawares. The famous loyalist **Simon Girty** (**Katepacomen**), and his brother **James Girty**, commanded the Mingos, Wyandots, and Shawnees from the upper Mad River and Darby Creek towns.

Pennsylvania boys taken by the Indians in 1756, the adopted Mingo Simon Girty, Shawnee James Girty, and Delaware George Girty battled the Americans during the Revolutionary War. Simon, the most prominent, was 39 in 1780. After the war, he led Indians in many raids and battles, including Wabash. Although hated by the frontier settlers, he aided many American captives. At the risk of his own life, he repeatedly saved Kenton from death during his old friend's captivity. Girty later retired to a farm in Amherstburg, Ontario, where Kenton saved him from vengeful Kentucky militiamen during the War of 1812. This stone marks Girty's grave at the site of his farm. (Dale Benington)

OPPOSING FORCES

AMERICAN

Clark's army at Peckuwe consisted of ten scouts, 950 infantrymen and ten Illinois Regiment artillerymen with two guns captured at Vincennes. Seventy infantrymen were in two companies of the Illinois Regiment. The remaining 880 were in four Kentucky militia regiments.

Most of Clark's officers and soldiers wore hunting shirts of buckskin or linsey-woolsey over loincloths, thigh-high leggings, and buckskin moccasins. For close combat, they carried tomahawks and a variety of large knives. Their main weapons were Pennsylvania – soon to be called Kentucky – rifles, which fired lead balls of .40 to .50 caliber.

Minimally competent riflemen could hit a man at 100 yards. In a famous shot during the 1778 siege of Boonesborough, Daniel Boone hit at 250 yards the head of a British officer peeking over a log. The weapons, however, took nearly a minute to reload, and required frequent cleaning. Josiah Collins of Captain William Harrod's company thought it memorable that Captain John Morrison was able to fire his rifle 13 times at Peckuwe.

The army's artillerymen had a 6lb and a 4lb gun that Clark had captured in Vincennes. Firing three to four times a minute, they used at the battle munitions of two types. Against structures, they fired iron or lead balls, which would fly more than 1,500 yards if unobstructed. With a 1.5lb powder load, the 6lb gun projected 3.5in.-diameter balls weighing 6.375lb. Their impact created shock waves that caused log structures to collapse. The 4lb gun used a 1lb powder load to fire 3in.-diameter balls weighing 4.24lb.

Against Indian warriors, Clark's guns used grapeshot. The load consisted of nine iron balls, which were arranged in three tiers around a spindle rising from a wooden platform, and wrapped in cloth secured by a cord. The 6lb gun's grapeshot contained 1.623-caliber balls, and the 4lb gun's balls of 1.417 caliber. These large balls could kill men behind light cover 600 yards beyond the guns.

Clark's men were masters of their weapons, and could endure extraordinary levels of hunger, discomfort, and exhaustion. Most, moreover, had fought Indians many times before. They were, however, difficult to control, and lacked training in unit maneuvers. Their performance at Peckuwe would depend on the quality of the commanders who led them.

Clark's scouts included Daniel Boone, the most famous of American frontiersmen. Forty-six in 1780, he had explored the Kentucky wilderness from 1767 through 1774. When asked whether he had ever gotten lost in the western woods, he responded, "I can't say I was ever lost, but I was once bewildered for 3 days." This unfinished Chester Harding portrait, painted in 1820, depicts Boone at 85. (National Portrait Gallery, Smithsonian Institution)

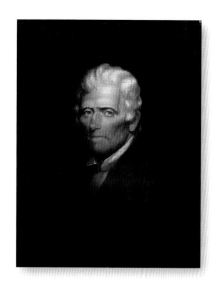

INDIAN

The 450-man Indian army had Shawnee, Delaware, Wyandot, and Mingo warriors. The Shawnees were from four subgroups: the Chalawgatha (also spelled Chillicothe), Kispoko, Mequachake, and Peckuwe (also spelled Piqua). The Delawares and Wyandots were from upper Mad River towns. The Mingos were from villages on Darby Creek. Also known as the Ohio Iroquois, they were members of tribes of the Iroquois confederacy who lived in Ohio.

Indian warriors wore loincloths, leggings, and moccasins, with feathers or porcupine quills decorating their hair, and rings in their ears and noses. Some wore hunting shirts like those of the Kentuckians. For battle, they covered their faces in terrifying designs with black, red, and white paint.

Both the Kentuckians and the Indians were capable of killing with their tomahawks at distances up to 10 yards. This young frontiersman is receiving expert instruction in throwing the weapon at the New Boston Fair, an annual re-enactment event held on the Peckuwe battlefield. (Author's photograph)

All had been trained from boyhood to endure discomfort, and to survive alone in the woods. The captive Margaret Pauley saw a young adopted Kentuckian being trained. Every morning during winter, 9-year-old John Calloway, who would lead a Kentucky regiment at Thames, was thrown into the freezing Mad River. "He had to take his morning plunge with the other Indians winter and summer," she remembered, "and frequently came into the cabin with icicles hanging to his hair. I always had a fire on hand for him."

The Indians had obtained by trading or raiding a variety of firearms, from the .75-caliber British Long Pattern Musket to trade muskets of as little as .45 caliber. Preferring smoothbore muskets to rifles, they fired from their weapons multiple projectiles, often loads of one large ball and three smaller balls of as little as .25 caliber.

Indians who lacked firearms, or had exhausted their powder or balls, used bows and arrows. The bows were from 4ft to 6ft long. The arrows were pointed with scrap metal or knapped stone. For close combat they used war clubs – often studded with pieces of metal or stone – tomahawks, and knives.

Indian warriors followed a way of war in which the goal was to exterminate enemies while suffering as few casualties as possible. All enemies, including women and children, were to be killed or captured. Captives who were not killed were enslaved or adopted. The Indians usually adopted captured children. They often adopted captured women, and, less frequently, adult males.

To minimize casualties, the Indians preferred raids against weak defenders to battles, and deceit and massacre to combat with enemies who could fight on even terms. They did not hesitate to use any stratagem that would allow enemies to be killed or captured without risk.

To deter aggression and demoralize enemies, the Indians conducted operations with a maximum of cruelty. By 1780, however, many had begun to oppose torture of prisoners. During the war, the Mequachake chief Biaseka shot a Kentuckian who was being burned.

Confident that they could defeat much larger American forces, Indian warriors fought with high morale. Before and after combat, they were uncontrollable. But in battle, they were very disciplined. Usually operating in units of about 20, they followed the commands of the man on the far right. Led by superb commanders, they skilfully executed the small-unit maneuvers that often decided frontier battles.

ORDERS OF BATTLE

(D) Detached; (K) Killed; (W) Wounded

AMERICAN ARMY (970)

Lieutenant-Colonel George Rogers Clark, Commander
Lieutenant-Colonel Benjamin Logan, Second in Command

COMPANY OF SPIES (10)

Captain Simon Kenton

ADVANCE GUARD (80)

Captain William Oldham, Commander
Lieutenant Bland Ballard, Second in Command (W)

ILLINOIS REGIMENT (3 companies) (80)

Lieutenant-Colonel George Rogers Clark, Commander
Major George Slaughter, Acting Commander
Company of Captain Benjamin Roberts (35)
Company of Captain Abraham Chaplin (35)
Artillery Company (10)
(One 6lb gun; one 4lb gun)
Lieutenant Richard Harrison, Commander

FLOYD'S REGIMENT (5 companies) (120)

Lieutenant-Colonel John Floyd, Commander
Company of Captain Parmena Briscoe (30)
Company of Captain Robert Johnson (15)
Company of Captain George Oins (20)
Company of Captain Charles Polk (20)
Company of Captain Henry Prather (35)

LINN'S REGIMENT (10 companies) (235)

Lieutenant-Colonel William Linn, Commander
Major Edward Bulger, Second in Command
Company of Captain Daniel Hall (15)
Company of Captain William Haskins (W) (15)
Company of Captain Lewis Hickman (K) (20)
Company of Captain Hardy Hill (15)
Company of Captain Michael Humble (20)
Company of Captain William McClure (35)
Company of Captain William Oldham (D) (25)
Lieutenant Joseph Brown, Acting Commander
Company of Captain James Patton (40)
Company of Captain Peter Sturgis (30)
Company of Captain John Swan (20)

HARROD'S REGIMENT (8 companies) (130)

Lieutenant-Colonel James Harrod, Commander
Company of Captain John Allison (15)
Company of Captain Squire Boone (10)
Company of Captain Robert Elliston (15)
Company of Captain William Harrod (20)
Company of Captain William McAfee (K) (20)
Company of Captain Hugh McGary (20)
Company of Captain Joseph McMurtry (W) (15)
Company of Captain John Morrison (W) (15)

LOGAN'S REGIMENT (6 companies) (235)

Lieutenant-Colonel Benjamin Logan, Commander
Company of Captain William Hays (25)
Company of Captain John Logan (30)
Company of Captain John Holder (40)
Company of Captain John Kennedy (30)
Company of Captain Robert Patterson (80)
Company of Captain William Whitley (30)

REARGUARD (80)

Unknown commander

INDIAN ARMY (450)

Black Hoof, Commander

CHALAWGATHA AND LOWER MAD RIVER SHAWNEES (300)

Commanders: Black Fish, Black Snake, Wryneck, Silver Heels

DELAWARES (30)

Buckongahelas, Commander

UPPER MAD RIVER SHAWNEES, MINGOS, AND WYANDOTS (120)

Commanders: Simon and James Girty

OPPOSING PLANS

AMERICAN

Clark believed that operations on the Ohio River frontier should be focused on achieving the American strategic objective, securing for the United States a border on the Great Lakes and the Mississippi River. Only the capture of Detroit, he thought, could finally attain that goal. It would end the ability of the British to use the Ohio Indians against the western settlers.

Clark considered the Indians an enemy who had already defeated themselves. Twenty years before, the Great Spirit had warned the famous Delaware shaman Neolin in a vision that, if the Indians addicted themselves to goods they did not make, they would perish. Now, despite their prowess in battle, they had become warriors who fought with weapons they must obtain from others.

When the British were expelled from Detroit, the Indians' sole sources of manufactured goods would be American. Until that occurred, however, they would continue their efforts to drive the settlers from the frontier. On the upper Ohio, the Americans were too well established for the Indians to succeed. But in Kentucky, the threat was serious; and, if Kentucky was lost, the war would end without the western border Clark was determined to establish.

Although a campaign against the Indians was necessary to maintain the Kentuckians' morale, it was unlikely to end raiding. When attacked, the Indians could easily decline battle, retreat to fight another day, and rebuild any destroyed villages. They had, however, a weakness. The Indians ate corn raised in fields around their villages. When the corn was nearly ready for harvest, it provided a fixed target to attack.

The target of Clark's campaign would be the ripening corn at Chalawgatha and nearby Peckuwe. Its destruction would force the Indians to abandon their bases for raiding, and move to sites farther from Kentucky. To survive the following winter, moreover, they would have to

Clark had no accurate map of his area of operations. John Filson's 1784 "Map of Kentucke" was the first cartographic work showing the locations of the settlements, roads, and trails in Kentucky. (Library of Congress, Geography and Map Division)

The Kentucky Frontier.

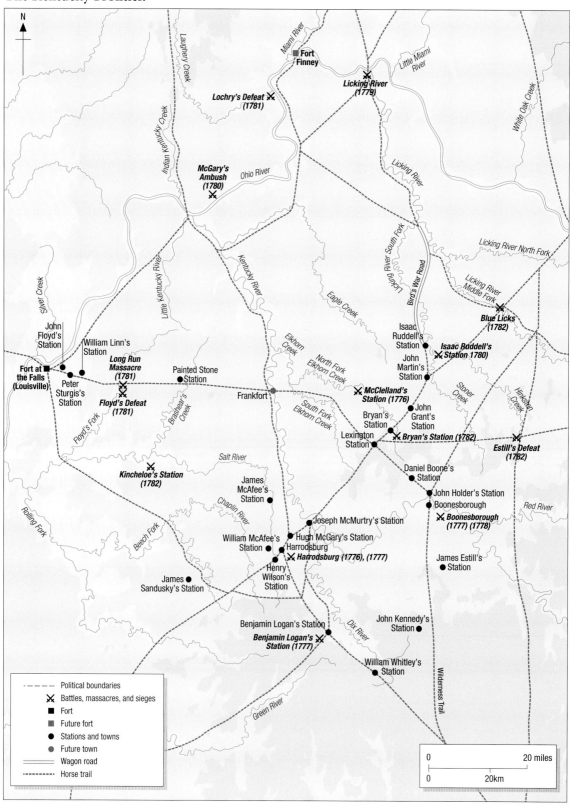

N

Lochry's Defeat (1781)

Fort Finney

Licking River (1779)

McGary's Ambush (1780)

Miami River

Little Miami River

White Oak Creek

Laughery Creek

Indian Kentucky Creek

Ohio River

Licking River

Licking River South Fork

Licking River North Fork

Licking River Middle Fork

Bird's War Road

Blue Licks (1782)

John Floyd's Station

William Linn's Station

Long Run Massacre (1781)

Painted Stone Station

Fort at the Falls (Louisville)

Peter Sturgis's Station

Floyd's Defeat (1781)

Silver Creek

Little Kentucky River

Kentucky River

Eagle Creek

Elkhorn Creek

North Fork Elkhorn Creek

Isaac Ruddell's Station

Isaac Buddell's Station 1780

John Martin's Station

Stoner Creek

Hinkson Creek

Frankfort

South Fork Elkhorn Creek

McClelland's Station (1776)

John Grant's Station

Bryan's Station

Bryan's Station (1782)

Lexington Station

Estill's Defeat (1782)

Brashear's Creek

Floyd's Fork

Salt River

Kincheloe's Station (1782)

James McAfee's Station

Chaplin River

Daniel Boone's Station

John Holder's Station

Boonesborough

Boonesborough (1777) (1778)

Red River

Rolling Fork

Beech Fork

Joseph McMurtry's Station

William McAfee's Station

Hugh McGary's Station

Harrodsburg

Harrodsburg (1776), (1777)

Henry Wilson's Station

James Estill's Station

James Sandusky's Station

John Kennedy's Station

Benjamin Logan's Station

Benjamin Logan's Station (1777)

Dix River

William Whitley's Station

Wilderness Trail

Green River

Legend

- - - - Political boundaries
- ✕ Battles, massacres, and sieges
- ■ Fort
- ■ Future fort
- ● Stations and towns
- ● Future town
- ═══ Wagon road
- · · · · Horse trail

0   20 miles

0   20km

ask the British for food. That humiliation would force them to accept that they could not long oppose the Americans without British aid.

The Indians, Clark thought, would attack his army as it advanced. They were unlikely to fight a defensive battle at the towns, where they could not easily apply their usual tactics. But in case they did, Clark would bring artillery to reduce any defensive structures the Indians might use.

INDIAN

Eighteenth-century frontier battles were fought by men with limited supplies of balls and powder against enemies dispersed in dense woods, which provided excellent cover and lines of retreat. Casualties in such battles depended less on the numbers engaged than on the tactics used. When 4,500 Americans, Indians, and British rangers met at Newtown in 1779, the casualties of both sides totaled only 28 dead and 48 wounded.

When, however, Indian tactics were successfully applied, comparatively large casualties might be inflicted in even small frontier engagements. From centuries of experience of war in the woods, the Indians had learned how to attain the most favorable ratio of enemy to friendly casualties. They achieved it by ambushing enemy forces, or attacking and encircling them.

The Indians were experts at planning and maximizing the effect of ambushes. At McMechen's Narrows, for example, Half King's Wyandots left valuable goods ahead of the Americans, who, when they paused to examine them, became stationary targets. The Mingos grudgingly admired a famous ambush by Catawbas from South Carolina. Three Catawba warriors with carved buffalo hooves left tracks near a Mingo hunting camp. When Mingo hunters followed the tracks into an ambush, the Catawbas allowed one to escape. Many Mingos then raced after the ambushers, and found waiting on the trail sharpened cane sticks tipped with rattlesnake venom, and a larger force of Catawbas. The adopted Mingo James Smith later watched a wary hunter search the ground around buffalo tracks. "He went very cautious until we found some fresh buffalo dung," Smith remembered. "He then smiled and said 'Catawba cannot make so.'"

When the Indians attacked, they always attempted to encircle even much larger enemy forces. The surrounded enemy then would suffer disproportionate casualties in its efforts to escape. Such attacks were most effective when launched against men not formed into battle units. They often were conducted against encamped enemies at dawn.

The Indians would ignore Clark's advance until they had assembled a force large enough to fight him. They then would follow the guidance of their shamans in planning a specific operation. Using magical methods of obtaining intelligence about the future, the shamans would determine the location and timing of an ambush or attack that would be successful.

A year after Peckuwe, Samuel Brady would demonstrate at the October 12, 1781 Battle of Brady Lake how 41 Americans using Indian tactics could inflict on an Indian force as many casualties as 3,000 Americans at Newtown. Brady and 40 of his rangers tracked 60 Wyandot raiders to a camp near what is now Kent, Ohio. After leaving 28 of his men 400 yards behind, Brady and the other 12 took up positions at night overlooking the camp. At dawn, they fired on the Indians and fled. A reckless pursuit of the 13 Americans led the Indians into an ambush by the other 28. In the engagement, Brady's men killed or wounded more than half of the Wyandots without suffering any casualties. The photograph shows the site of Brady's most celebrated feat. At what is now Brady's Leap Park in Kent, he later in 1781 escaped pursuing Indians by a 22ft leap between cliffs overlooking the Cuyahoga River. (Public domain)

The Ohio Indians.

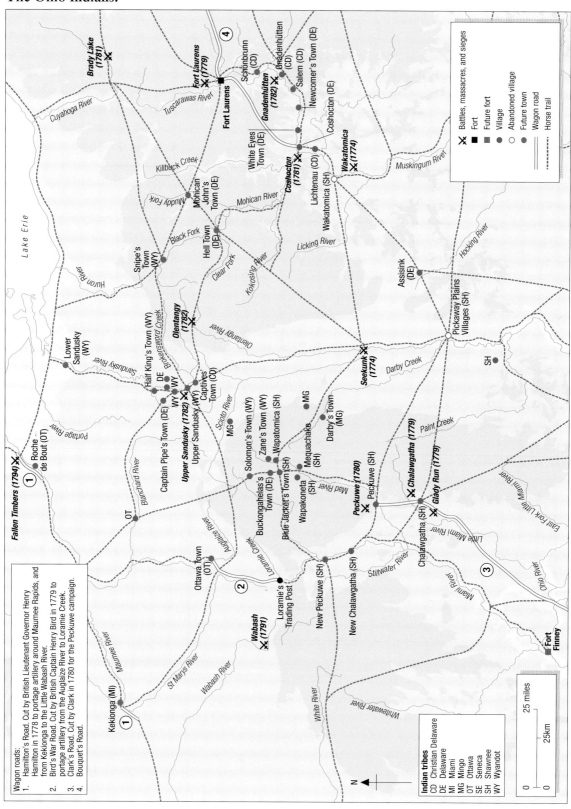

Battles, massacres, and sieges ✕✕
Fort ◼
Future fort ◼
Village ●
Abandoned village ○
Future town ●
Wagon road
Horse trail

Wagon roads:
1. Hamilton's Road. Cut by British Lieutenant Governor Henry Hamilton in 1778 to portage artillery around Maumee Rapids, and from Kekionga to the Little Wabash River.
2. Bird's War Road. Cut by British Captain Henry Bird in 1779 to portage artillery from the Auglaize River to Loramie Creek.
3. Clark's Road. Cut by Clark in 1780 for the Peckuwe campaign.
4. Bouquet's Road.

Indian tribes
CD Christian Delaware
DE Delaware
MI Miami
MG Mingo
OT Ottawa
SE Seneca
SH Shawnee
WY Wyandot

0 ___ 25 miles
0 ___ 25km

N

THE CAMPAIGN

ORIGINS

The winter that arrived in late 1779 was the worst ever seen on the Ohio River frontier. As Indian warriors desperately searched for game to feed their women and children, 4ft of snow blocked the Cumberland Gap, and 2ft of ice covered the Kentucky River. It was, Floyd wrote on February 20, 1780, "the severest winter that ever was known."

The settlers huddled around the fires in their cabins were optimistic about what the new year would bring. Many had worried that they would never own the land on which they had settled. Title to land in western Virginia could be obtained only by warrants issued by the state. Such warrants granted acreage and directed county surveyors to determine deed boundaries in a location chosen by the warrant holder.

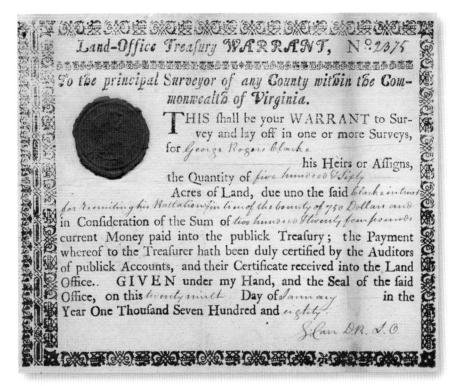

This January 27, 1780 warrant for 560 acres was one of 300 sent to Clark for his Illinois Regiment soldiers. (Special Collections Research Center, University of Chicago Library)

Virginia had granted for service in the French and Indian War, in Lord Dunmore's War, and in the Illinois Regiment, warrants for areas of its western territory. It also sold warrants to land speculators. But none were issued merely for settling in the West.

As Clark had waited at Vincennes for Bowman's men, Virginia had enacted new legislation to encourage settlement on the frontier. Under the Virginia Land Law of 1779, the early settlers now could obtain warrants. And a commission to issue warrants was to be sent to Kentucky.

Three weeks after Licking River, a commission led by Colonel William Fleming, who had been grievously wounded leading a regiment at Point Pleasant, had begun hearing at Logan's Station the claims of men who already held Virginia warrants for land grants in Kentucky. In 1780, the commission would begin granting warrants for early settlement. Many who had fled from the Indians' attacks would return to obtain warrants establishing their claims. Others would come to buy warrants. Still others would arrive to survey the areas granted. Thousands, perhaps, would come.

When the snow began to melt in 1780, Clark received orders from Jefferson, the new governor of Virginia. He was to secure the Mississippi border by building a strong fortress at the mouth of the Ohio River. Soon thereafter, the settlers at Boonesborough, Lexington, and Bryan's Station sent petitions asking Clark to lead them against Chalawgatha. On April 4, Clark declined.

Ten days later, Clark went down the Ohio to build what he would name Fort Jefferson. The settlers' disappointment then quickly passed. On April 16, Fleming's commissioners began hearing early settlers' claims at Henry Wilson's new station near Harrodsburg.

In London, Germain was hopeful about 1780 too. Since Burgoyne's disaster at Saratoga, nearly every day had brought bad news. Spain had joined France in the war against Britain. Island after island in the Caribbean had fallen. Gibraltar was besieged. Supported by the French, the Mahrattas and Hyder Ali, ruler of Mysore, were threatening to drive the British out of India.

Britain had done comparatively little in North America for two years. But in 1780, the British would implement a new strategy devised by Germain.

The appearance today of the mouth of the Ohio River (left) as it reaches the Mississippi (right), looking toward Kentucky from Illinois. (Photograph by C. Bradford Crenshaw)

Fort Pontchartrain, built by the French in 1701, guarded Detroit until 1779, when the British began constructing larger Fort Lernoult. Both usually were called Fort Detroit. This marker at the corner of Shelby and West Fort streets in Detroit indicates the site of the southwest bastion of Fort Lernoult. (Dale Benington)

They would attack the American hinterland, where large numbers of loyalists continued to support the crown, and take advantage of the Spanish decision to enter the war. Four armies would suppress the rebellion by attacking from unexpected directions, the south and the west.

The largest, led by Brigadier-General the Earl Cornwallis, would take Charleston in South Carolina. As loyalists from Georgia and the Carolinas swelled its ranks, the Cherokees would attack the American settlements. After ending resistance in the southern backcountry, Cornwallis would march north to occupy Virginia.

Another army, commanded by Major-General John Campbell, would capture Spanish New Orleans. It would proceed up the Mississippi River to seize Kaskaskia, Cahokia, and St Louis, and then move east to reduce the American settlements west of the Appalachians.

Major Arent de Peyster, an American who had chosen a career as an officer in the British 8th Regiment of Foot, now commanded in Detroit. The able de Peyster was to organize the third and fourth armies, which would support Campbell's operation. The prominent fur trader Emmanuel Hesse would lead 1,000 Indians down the Mississippi to attack St Louis, Cahokia, and Kaskaskia from the north. At the same time, Bird would march from Detroit with 150 Canadian militiamen and 100 Indians, taking with him 6lb and 3lb guns. After joining another 600 warriors at the mouth of the Miami River, he would reduce the Kentuckians' forts and stations.

On April 26, Chaplin made a daring escape from Upper Sandusky to warn the Kentuckians of Bird's invasion. By then, more than 1,000 men were camped at Wilson's Station. Some, like 30-year-old Isaac Shelby, who had distinguished himself leading a company at Point Pleasant, and 26-year-old Thomas Vickroy, who would fight at Peckuwe, had come to begin work as surveyors.

Three days after Chaplin's escape, Clark arrived at the mouth of the Ohio. As his men began building Fort Jefferson, Clark's mind was on Detroit. In

1779, he could have taken it easily. Now the western center of British power was protected by a stronger fort and larger garrison.

A barrier more formidable than its walls and defenders, however, also now guarded the British stronghold. Many in Virginia would object to any Detroit campaign proposed by Clark because of the cost. Since 1777, he had been sending back to Virginia accounts of his expenses. Operations on the remote frontier required long periods of militia service, which was compensated by the day. Transporting supplies hundreds of miles across the mountains, moreover, required a monumental outlay.

The cost of Clark's operations, Jefferson had written, had shocked the legislators in Williamsburg. Some thought there must be fraud. It would take time, the Virginia governor had said, to muster sufficient support for him to authorize an attack by Clark on the British base.

Jefferson's authorization, however, would not be enough. Like the men in Clark's Illinois Regiment, who had received no pay since their enlistment, the merchants who had furnished Clark's supplies had never been compensated. Now they were demanding payment in advance, and they were insisting on payment in hard currency.

The hard currencies available in America were English pounds and Spanish dollars, which traded at 30 dollars to a pound. To finance the war, Congress and each of the states had issued currencies that guaranteed redemption in pounds or dollars, but their insolvent governments could not honor the guarantees. When he had recaptured Vincennes a year before, suppliers had been willing to take eight Virginia dollars for a Spanish dollar. Now they wanted 77, if they would take Virginia dollars at all. Vigo was advancing as many Spanish dollars as he could, but his resources were limited.

Another season of Indian raiding had begun. By May 1, Indians had killed more than 40 settlers at homesteads southwest of Pittsburgh, and they had made it impossible for the surveyors to work in Kentucky. "I took my compass and chain," remembered Vickroy, "to make a fortune by surveying, but when we got there, the Indians wouldn't let us survey."

Campbell's campaign foundered. But on May 2, Hesse's warriors began moving down the Mississippi. When de Leyba received warning of Hesse's approach, he sent a message to Clark, asking him to hasten up the Mississippi. As de Leyba's Spanish messenger went down the river on May 19, Chaplin reached Louisville. The settlers at the Falls immediately dispatched their own messenger, asking Clark to return.

When Clark reached St Louis on May 25, de Leyba offered him command of the 29 Spanish regulars, 251 militiamen, and five guns available to defend the Upper Louisiana capital. After declining, Clark hurried to nearby Cahokia. That same day, Bird's men and guns left Detroit in a flotilla of watercraft for the invasion of Kentucky. With him went Girty, McKee, Elliott, and Blue Jacket.

As Bird's men sailed up the Maumee River on May 26, Hesse's Indians arrived at their targets. Seven hundred attacked St Louis. From a stone tower built at unfinished Fort San Carlos, and buildings in the town, the defenders repelled them. The frustrated attackers then directed their rage at any unprotected settlers they could find. They ultimately killed or captured 92.

Three hundred more Indians attacked Cahokia. But Clark had hastily deployed to defend the town 100 men and a 6lb gun he had taken at Vincennes. After firing a few shots, Hesse's Indians departed.

Reinforcements from Kaskaskia soon arrived in Cahokia. Furious that supposedly neutral Fox and Sauk warriors had joined Hesse's attack, Clark dispatched Captain John Montgomery and 230 men on a retaliatory raid against their villages on the Illinois River. He then returned to the mouth of the Ohio.

As Clark went down the Mississippi, Bird's men continued up the Maumee, and then the Auglaize River. From the Auglaize, they cut a road for the artillery to Loramie's Trading Post, and then paddled down Loramie Creek and the Miami River toward the Ohio.

Waiting to join Bird at the mouth of the Miami, hundreds of Indians were roaming the northern Kentucky woods. Floyd was afraid to go even the 6 miles from his station to Louisville. "Hardly one week passes," he wrote on

The St Louis and Cahokia settlers responded to Hesse's campaign in two expeditions against the nearest British stronghold, small Fort St Joseph, in what is now Niles, MI. The first, by Jean-Baptiste Hamelin and 30 Cahokia men, ended in disaster at the December 5, 1780 Battle of Trail Creek. The second, by Captain Eugenio Pierro and 100 St Louis and Cahokia militiamen and Indian allies, destroyed the fortress on February 12, 1781. This Stephen Walsh illustration from Alejandro de Quesada's *Spanish Colonial Fortifications in North America, 1565–1822*, shows the appearance of the stone tower at Fort San Carlos. (© Osprey Publishing Ltd)

As Clark was returning from Fort Jefferson to Louisville, a new Indian fighter appeared on the upper Ohio. When three raiders opened fire on a party of American pursuers, all but 16-year-old Lewis Wetzel fled. In his first battle with Indians, Wetzel then killed all three. For the next 15 years, he would track raiders far into Ohio, kill them with impunity, and become known to the Indians as "the Death Wind." This 1888 photograph shows the site of Wetzel's first combat, now lost Wetzel's Spring, near St Clairsville, OH. (Author's collection)

May 30, "without someone being scalped between this and the Falls and I have almost got too cowardly to travel about without company."

On June 4, Clark arrived back at Fort Jefferson. The next day, the messenger from Louisville reached him. Clark left immediately with two men. To avoid ambush on the river, they began a 250-mile-long trip to the Falls through the woods.

As Clark hurried back to the Falls, stunning news reached the Kentuckians. On May 12, the British had captured Charleston, and the 5,000-man American army defending it. Now Cornwallis was marching north. Loyalists were flocking to join him, and the Cherokees were attacking the most exposed frontier settlements. When Bedinger and Shelby heard the news, they and many others went down the Wilderness Trail to join the fight.

After Bird's army finally assembled at the mouth of the Miami, he, McKee, Elliott, and the Indian war leaders began planning the invasion. They should first attack Clark's fort at the Falls, Bird proposed. When silence followed, McKee knew the reason. Clark was not there, he reassured the Indians. The Kentucky commander was at the mouth of the Ohio.

But Clark was now a legendary figure, one who appeared where he was not expected. "The Indians," McKee wrote to de Peyster, "could not be prevailed upon." They would instead, the chiefs insisted, attack the central Kentucky settlements.

After moving up the Ohio, and then the Licking River, Bird's men halted on June 20 at the Forks of the Licking, where the stream ceased to be navigable. There they began to cut through the woods a 45-mile-long path that would be remembered as Bird's War Road. It led to Ruddell's Station. Also known as Fort Liberty, it was after Harrodsburg the largest settlement in Kentucky.

On June 24, Bird's army reached Ruddell's Station. His overwhelming numbers did not intimidate the 49 militiamen stationed there, nor the fort's more than 250 settlers. But then, to their horror, the Kentuckians saw Bird's 6lb gun, which could level their fortress' walls.

Girty appeared at the station's gate to demand surrender. Isaac Ruddell then invited Bird and McKee into the fort to discuss terms. He told the Americans, Bird reported to de Peyster, "that their lives should be saved and themselves taken to Detroit." But, he added, "I forewarned them that the savages would adopt some of their children."

The Indians had promised Bird that they would not enter the fort until the next day. They had also agreed not to kill the settlers' cattle, with which the British commander planned to feed his men. But they were eager to collect scalps and prisoners, and to gorge themselves in a feast.

"Whilst Captain McKee and myself were in the fort settling these matters with the poor people," Bird reported to de Peyster, "they rushed in, tore the poor children from their mothers' breasts, killed a wounded man and every one of the cattle." "The Indians came rushing in," remembered the settler James Trabue, "and plundered the people and they even stripped their clothes off them and divided the prisoners among the Indians. In a few minutes the man did not know where his wife or child was, nor the wife know where her husband or either of her children was, nor the children where their parents or brothers or sisters were." "Some 20," remembered the settler James Morrow, "were tomahawked in cold blood."

On June 26, Clark reached Louisville, where Major George Slaughter had arrived from Virginia with 50 welcome reinforcements for the Illinois Regiment. No British and Indian army was anywhere near the Falls, he was told. That same day, Bird's men advanced another 6 miles to Martin's Station, which immediately surrendered. There the Indians again killed the cattle.

Robert Patterson's cabin in Lexington is preserved on the grounds of Transylvania University. (Courtesy of Transylvania University)

This monument is at the site of Ruddell's Station, about 3 miles south of Cynthiana, KY. (Photograph by Les Daugherty)

On June 27, as Clark was hurrying on toward central Kentucky, the Indians went 8 miles further to Grant's Station, where they killed two before the settlers fled. Next would come Bryan's Station, 5 miles beyond Grant's. But a rumor then spread that Clark was coming with an army. The Indians, Bird remembered, "proposed returning." His food almost exhausted, the British commander was compelled to order a retreat. His army, the frustrated Bird wrote to de Peyster, "could have gone through the whole country without any opposition had the Indians preserved the cattle."

A huge British and Indian army was coming, said the Grant's Station settlers when they reached Bryan's Station. The settlers there joined their flight. Their numbers swelled as they fled through Lexington, McMurtry's Station, and McGary's.

When the column of terrified Kentuckians reached Harrodsburg, Kenton went back up the trail to investigate. There was no one at Martin's Station, he reported. At Ruddell's, there were "a number of people lying about killed and scalped." And further down the Licking, he had seen the attackers marching back toward the Ohio River with hundreds of prisoners.

The Kentuckians had displayed great ingenuity in surviving the hardships of life in their isolated habitat. Anna Pogue, who had carried west a spinning wheel, had found that nettle lint and buffalo hair could be cross-woven to create a durable cloth for dresses and hunting shirts. Another settler had learned how to make rope from pawpaw bark. Still another had found that a rifle was more effective if the powder in its barrel was behind a wad, a greased patch of cloth.

The settlers had also endured heartbreak with grim fortitude. Again and again, they had buried the bodies left by the raiders. They had mourned their dead. And they had prayed for those the Indians had taken.

But this was too much. Without warning, the wilderness had claimed more than 400 people who, like them, had thought themselves safe when behind their stations' wooden walls. A month before, raiders had killed William Bryan. Now his three brothers announced that they and their families were abandoning Bryan's Station. At Wilson's Station, some planned to leave for Virginia as soon as they got their warrants. Others thought it wiser to depart immediately.

When Clark arrived in Harrodsburg, every eye turned to the 6ft-tall figure with flaming red hair. "The great panic occasioned through Kentucky by the taking of Ruddell's and Martin's Stations," remembered the settler John Bradford, "caused the people to look to Clark as their only hope. His counsel and advice were received as coming from an oracle."

THE ADVANCE TO THE OHIO RIVER

The 27-year-old commander of a Virginia militia regiment held no official position in Kentucky. He nonetheless immediately began giving orders. Clark issued them, remembered John McCaddon, "on his own authority," and they were, McCaddon recalled, "promptly obeyed."

No one was going to leave Kentucky, Clark announced, dispatching guards to block the Wilderness Trail. The land claims proceedings were canceled until further notice. Every man in the settlements, regardless of why he was there, now would fight. One in five would remain to guard the women and children. The rest would meet him at the mouth of the Licking River on July 31. Then he would lead them across the Ohio to attack the Shawnees.

On July 2, an excited Clark arrived back in Louisville. He had 29 days to assemble at the rendezvous point men from locations as far as 140 miles away. He had 18 to obtain food and supplies for them, and watercraft, wagons, and horses for transport. And to get what he needed, he could give only promises of future payment by Virginia.

That same day, Bird's dwindling army reached the mouth of the Miami. Girty, McKee, Elliott, Blue Jacket, and most of the Indians had left, taking

The Ohio River today. (Craig Stihler, US Fish and Wildlife Service)

Many of the women who would remain at the settlements were capable Indian fighters. One was Whitley's wife, ranked by some the best rifle shot in Kentucky. At the time of the battle, Esther Whitley was pregnant with their fifth child. The photograph shows August Leinbach's 1928 "Madonna of the Trail" in Springfield, OH. (Photograph by Lorie Arendt)

with them about 200 captives. Isaac and Elizabeth Ruddell remained. But the Indians had taken 12-year-old son Stephen and three other Ruddell children. John and Rachel Loveless from Martin's Station also were still with Bird's army. But 15-year-old Sarah Loveless and her four younger brothers and sisters had been carried off as well.

The Indians who had left Bird soon reached Chalawgatha, where they displayed their scalps and prisoners. Most then went on to Peckuwe and towns further up the Mad River. When Girty, McKee, and Elliott reached Wapatomica on July 8, McKee sent a report to de Peyster. He had asked the Shawnees, he wrote, to send warriors to watch for movement by Clark up the Ohio River.

At every station and homestead in Kentucky, the men began deciding who would go and who would stay. At Painted Creek Station, remembered McCaddon, "We cast lots who should go, and unanimously chose Squire Boone as our captain, making in all thirteen in number." At James McAfee's Station, his nephew Robert was told, they decided to leave "six or seven men only besides their women and children."

At the Falls, Clark was constantly receiving messages from the men who would be his senior commanders. Slaughter would bring two Illinois Regiment infantry companies, and an artillery company with a 6lb and a 4lb gun. Floyd and Linn were organizing two regiments from the Louisville area. Logan and James Harrod were assembling two more from central Kentucky.

How many men he would have remained uncertain. No one knew how many there were in Kentucky, nor how many would be able to evade Clark's guards. And there also were many loyalists. The party with which he had traveled to Kentucky in 1779, remembered William Clinkenbeard of Captain John Holder's company, had been "all grand Tories, pretty nigh."

He might have 1,000, Clark guessed. But that number would not ensure success. At Point Pleasant, he knew, 1,100 frontiersmen had narrowly escaped defeat by Cornstalk's 700 Indians, losing 80 dead and 140 wounded. If Bird's army was still intact, he would face a formidable enemy. Even if not, the Indians might have enough time to assemble an army as large as Cornstalk's. To avoid a disaster like Bowman's, he would need artillery, and cutting a road for the guns and munitions wagon would slow his advance.

The stakes, moreover, were enormous. If his army were defeated, many of his men would never reach the Ohio River. Even if it prevailed, casualties like those at Point Pleasant might cause the disheartened settlers to abandon Kentucky.

As Clark labored ceaselessly at the Falls, distracting news arrived from Vincennes. The famous French cavalry officer Augustin Mottin de la Balme was there recruiting settlers to fight the British. But they would not fight as Americans. Reminding the settlers of their heritage, de la Balme had raised as his army's standard the fleur-de-lis of France. Still more French settlers would join them when they reached Detroit, he proclaimed. Then yet more would rise against the British in Montreal and Quebec. France's lost North American empire would be reclaimed.

Clark, however, had no time to address the French officer's activities. As he labored to obtain food and supplies, he received frequent reports on who would cross the Ohio with him. Success, he knew, would depend on the quality of his scouts and unit commanders.

Slowed by the need to build a road, his army would not be able to advance rapidly. Its fate would turn on the ability of his scouts to warn against surprise attacks. Boone, he learned, was going, and Kenton too. Unlike Boone, Kenton could not read or write. But to such men, their environment was a virtual newspaper, full of stories about recent events. In broken branches and stems, trodden grass, and prints in mud, dirt, and dust, they could read the number, size, and weight of those who had passed, the speed at which they had moved, and how recently they had left their marks.

His almost uncontrollable men, he thought, would fight formidable enemies widely dispersed in woods. To prevail, they would need leaders who would exercise good judgment when he was not with them. The Kentuckians would falter under commanders like Bowman, who would panic in a crisis, or McGary, ever determined to prove that he was fearless. To Clark's relief, he learned that he would have many that he had hoped for. Ballard and Chaplin would be with Slaughter. Wells was coming as a lieutenant in one of Floyd's companies. Bulger would be Linn's second in command, and Oldham would lead one of his companies. Whitley would command one of Logan's.

From the Falls, messengers carried a flurry of orders. Floyd, Linn, Harrod, and Logan were to divide their companies into messes of about six men. Each mess must have a packhorse to carry the men's blankets, munitions, supplies, and food, and also an axe and large kettle. Linn was to have Captain Peter Sturgis get the boats they would need. Logan was to bring as many extra packhorses as he could find.

As the hot July days passed, still more messengers sped from Louisville. Harrod was to send McGary's and Captain John Allison's companies to the Falls. Hunting up the Ohio, they would amass a supply of meat at the mouth of the Kentucky River, where the rest of Harrod's regiment would join them. Slaughter's, Floyd's, and Linn's men would march up the south bank of the Ohio as a flotilla of small boats carried the army's guns and supplies to the mouth of the Kentucky. They and Harrod's men would then continue upriver to the mouth of the Licking. Logan and the companies raised near his station were to meet his other companies at Bryan's Station. From there, his regiment would march down the Licking to join the rest of the army.

Soon those who would stay behind began leaving their small stations and homesteads for safer strongholds. With them went their cattle, pigs, and chickens, and horses carrying their most valuable possessions: firearms, plowshares, and iron tools; seeds; and documents, family bibles, and heirlooms.

De la Balme was the author of widely used manuals on horsemanship and cavalry tactics. On November 15, 1780, Miamis led by Little Turtle attacked the French officer and his 104 men near present Churubusco, IN, killing or capturing them all. This J. M. Moreau engraving from de la Balme's 1773 *Essais sur l'equitation* illustrates proper posture while mounted. (Author's collection)

Those who would go began preparing for what they would face. William Harrod, who would lead the company from his brother's station, was among the worried. He "dreamed before leaving Harrodsburg," his son remembered, "that he would either be killed or wounded, but rather than remain and be considered a coward, he went along taking bandages with him."

McGary's and Allison's companies were the first to march. After they reached the Falls, Henry Wilson of Allison's company led them up the Ohio. As they moved upriver, Logan's men marched north toward Bryan's Station, adding more companies as they went.

On July 20, Clark's flotilla left Louisville. It consisted, remembered Wilson, of "two or three old keelboats, and several skiffs and perogues." The watercraft carried with the 6lb and 4lb guns the fruits of his frantic logistical labor. He somehow had amassed an ample supply of munitions, 375 bushels of corn, 3,130lb of flour, and 40 bushels of salt.

Staying close to the south bank of the river, where Slaughter's, Floyd's, and Linn's men hunted and the packhorses grazed, Clark's boats went up the Ohio. On July 23, they found Harrod and the rest of his regiment waiting at the mouth of the Kentucky River. That same day, Logan arrived at Bryan's Station. There he found the companies he had expected, but not all the men. Three days before, he was told, John Clairy of the Bryan's Station company had saddled a horse and ridden away.

As Logan's full regiment marched toward the Licking River on July 24, Bird's army and its hungry prisoners reached Ottawa Town on the Auglaize. For even the strong, the march had been a trial. Twenty-four-year-old Leonhard Kratz had been made to carry a massive kettle. John and Thomas Mahan had taken turns bearing their aged father on their backs. And Rachel Loveless had borne on her back her 2-year-old son Joseph.

For some of the old, it had been a death march. Trabue remembered how Mrs John Burger had died: "As one company of Indians marched along, this old woman behind, one Indian behind her would jump up and wave his tomahawk and cut a number of capers. The blow came when this old lady was not expecting it. They finished her and scalped her."

Many of the young had died too. The Indians had killed Kratz's infant son Peter when he had made too much noise. Rachel Loveless had lost her crying infant too. But she had been able to keep Joseph quiet, and stayed silent herself as the starving toddler gnawed ever deeper into her shoulder.

That same day, scouting Shawnee warriors discovered Clark's advance up the Ohio at present Vevay, IN. Most of the Kentuckians had stayed south of the river, but McGary and 30 men had sought better hunting on the north bank. The Indians waited until the approach of sunset, when the hunters began entering their boats to recross the river. Then they opened fire, killing nine and wounding more.

The Kentuckians across the Ohio responded. "Five hundred guns," remembered John Sandusky, "were shot from the Kentucky shore when the Indians attacked." As boatfuls of men

After fighting in a Hessian Regiment at Saratoga, Leonhard Kratz had escaped from a prisoner-of-war camp in Virginia in 1779, and found refuge with the German immigrant Wilhelm Munger, who was traveling with his family to Kentucky. He then married Munger's daughter Mary, and settled at Ruddell's Station. Leonhard and Mary Munger survived the march, and years of servitude and separation. Ultimately reunited, they settled on a farm near modern Harrow, Ontario. These descendants of the Ruddell's and Martin's Station settlers, retracing in 2010 the first day of their ancestors' march to Detroit, are where Bird's War Road crossed the South Fork of the Licking. (Photograph by Keith Morris)

When Boone's eyesight began to fail in 1810, he purchased these spectacles. (Kentucky Historical Society, 1954.15)

began crossing the river to rescue the hunters, the Indians retired. "This little check," recalled Wilson, "put a stop to hunting on shore."

On July 25, the Kentuckians moved further up the Ohio. With no further prospect of eating game, they turned to the food on Clark's boats. They then discovered that water had leaked into the holds. All of the corn was spoiled, along with six of the 40 bushels of salt, and 1,500 of the 3,130lb of flour. The Kentuckians, Wilson remembered, "almost despaired of continuing the campaign."

As Logan's men marched down the Licking through an area famous for its profusion of buffalo, Clark's worried Kentuckians continued upriver. On July 30, Wilson remembered, they saw "a flat-bottomed boat, loaded with corn, and destined for the Falls of the Ohio to market." Clark seized the cargo. Virginia would pay, he told the outraged owner.

Late that afternoon, Clark's men reached the mouth of the Licking. There they found the bones of David Rogers and the men who had died ten months before, and, grazing among them, a saddled horse.

Cheering erupted the following day, when Logan's men arrived. "It was," remembered Captain James Patton of Linn's Regiment, "a delightful sight to see. All good woodsmen well armed with good rifles, and chiefly good marksmen."

Clark, who saw more mouths to feed, told the new arrivals about the loss of supplies. "We could have gotten buffalo meat and jerked it," remembered Clinkenbeard, "had we thought that we would have needed it or Clark would not have supplied us." But Logan's men were not discouraged. "They were," recalled Robert McAfee, "in high spirits and made no complaints as General Clark had done the best he could." "Not a single complaint was heard to escape the lips of a solitary individual," a surprised Bradford remembered.

But then the men from Bryan's Station recognized the saddled horse. It was Clairy's. He had been a loyalist, they realized, and he had deserted to warn the Indians that they were coming.

That night, the Kentuckians sat around their fires. As usual, Boone entertained his companions by reading from one of the two books he always carried, the Bible and *Gulliver's Travels*. But the mood was somber. "All," recalled Bradford, "appeared to be impressed with the belief that, if this little army was defeated, few would be able to escape, and the Indians then would fall on the defenseless women and children in Kentucky, and destroy the whole."

THE ADVANCE TO CHALAWGATHA

On August 1, the Kentuckians advanced beyond the Ohio. "Before the boats crossed over to the Indian side," the scout Abraham Thomas recalled, "Boone and myself were taken into the foremost boat and landed above a small cut in the bank, opposite the mouth of Licking. We were desired to spy through the woods for Indian signs. I was much younger than Boone, ran up the bank in great glee, and cut into a beech tree with my tomahawk, which I verily believe was the first tree cut into by a white man on the present site of Cincinnati."

Fifty-eight miles ahead, an alarmed Black Hoof, who had succeeded Black Fish as chief at Chalawgatha, had received reports from Clairy and the warriors who had ambushed McGary's men. "The Indians," remembered the captive Margaret Pauley, "knew of Clark's advance from the time he crossed the Ohio, and they seemed very much alarmed."

The Shawnee chief, who had fewer than 100 warriors, had sent messengers asking for aid. After reaching Peckuwe, they were already moving up the Mad River toward the Shawnee, Delaware, and Wyandot towns upstream, and the Mingo villages on Darby Creek. He also had asked the trader Peter Loramie, who had been in Chalawgatha, to take Clairy to Detroit. "The Indians," Loramie remembered, "beseeched me to conduct this deserter to Detroit and to tell their father (the commandant) about the trouble where they were." The need for haste, he recalled, "caused me to ride two horses to death along a route where one could not find any remount."

The arriving Kentuckians soon began forming Clark's first Ohio camp. Some began work on two cabins, where a 25-man garrison would guard the boats. "I helped to build the first house ever built on that ground," remembered McCaddon, "for I was at my post in guarding the artificers who did the labor of building."

The corn (maize) raised by the Indians and frontier settlers was what is now called "Indian corn." Its hard kernels were beaten into a coarse meal, which was used to make hominy, bread, or porridge. Blows to crush the kernels inspired the 19th-century American song "Jimmy Crack Corn." The photograph shows ears of Indian corn. (Author's photograph)

While McCaddon watched the woods, Clark was busy counting. There were enough balls, grapeshot, and powder; they would have more than 100 axes to cut the road; and there was a quart of corn per man, barely enough to keep the men alive until they reached the Chalawgatha cornfields.

But there were not enough horses. Twenty-four would be needed for the 6lb gun, the 4lb piece, and the munitions wagon. Each would need four horses, which would pull in half-day shifts. That left 150 horses, enough to pack the supplies, but too few for the food. The men would have to carry their own corn.

Clark ordered the food distributed. "We got just six quarts of corn," remembered Clinkenbeard. "Might parch, pound, bake, or do as we pleased with it, but that was what we were to get." The kernels were too hard for any but the strongest teeth. Soon the flat bits of hundreds of tomahawks were pounding on tree stumps. "We were like a parcel of young pigs just learning to crack corn," he recalled. "Went crack! crack!"

The Kentucky commander then met with his officers. They would advance to Chalawgatha, he said, and then to Peckuwe, 12 miles beyond on the Mad River, and they would march at dawn.

Kenton's scouts would go first. Some would advance about 2 miles ahead of the army, examining possible ambush sites and blazing the course of the trail to Chalawgatha. Others would scatter, and search for signs that Indians were in the area.

Behind the scouts would go the axe-wielding pioneers. Every day, 100 men would be detached from their companies to fell trees. Working in two-hour shifts, they would transform the trail into a road at least 15ft wide, and bridge any unfordable streams or impassable ravines.

Eighty men from Slaughter's, Floyd's, and Linn's companies would be permanently detached to serve as the army's advance guard. Oldham and Ballard would leave their companies to command the unit, which would march ahead of the main body of the army. Another 80 men, from Harrod's and Logan's companies, would form the rearguard, which would follow the army at the same distance.

Kenton carried with him to start fires this enameled tin box. The box, which contained flints and tinder, had in its cover a glass that could focus the sun's rays to ignite. Another cover protected the glass. (Kentucky Historical Society, 1977.15)

The guns, wagon, and packhorses would go forward on the road. The rest of the army would advance in four single-file columns about 40 yards apart, two on either side of the road. The companies in the far right and left column would detach guards, so that each would have 20 men about 100 yards beyond its exposed flank.

As they marched, the Indians might attack quickly from any direction. If they came from the front, the guns would go forward to support the advance guard. The two columns on the left would advance to form the Kentucky left wing, and the other two to form the Kentucky right. If the attack came from behind, the artillery would support the rearguard, and the left columns would form the Kentucky right, and the right columns the Kentucky left. If the Indians attacked from a flank, the two columns assaulted would hold their position. The guns would support them in the center, and the front and rear sections of the other two columns would advance to positions on their flanks.

The Indians also might attack while they were encamped. Their camps would be hollow rectangles enclosing about 25–30 acres. Guarding the guns, wagon, and packhorses in the center, companies would occupy assigned sections of the perimeter. As the army neared Chalawgatha, the numbers of sentries would each night be increased.

Long before dawn, Kenton, Boone, and the other scouts were moving up the trail by the light of a new moon. All knew the safety rules of their perilous craft. The greatest danger, each knew, was not that he would be seen, but that Indians would find and follow the signs he left behind as he moved. He must never go back on a path he took. Before halting to eat or rest, he must always circle back to a concealed point near the path, from which he could see any pursuers before he was seen.

At daybreak, the axes began felling trees. Soon they reached a fork in the trail, where the scouts had blazed the path to the right. "Our way," remembered Thomas, "lay over the uplands of an untracked, primitive forest, through which, with great labor, we cut and bridged a road for the accommodation of our pack horses and cannon."

A mile from the Ohio River, the Indian trail forked. The right path led to Chalawgatha, and the left to modern Hamilton, OH. This marker on East Central Parkway in Cincinnati is at the location. (Photograph by Dale Benington)

Caesar Creek took its name from the adopted Thawakila Shawnee Old Caesar. Once a slave in Virginia, he worked in Chalawgatha as a blacksmith before emigrating to Missouri in 1778. He left behind his son Young Caesar, who fought at Peckuwe. The photograph shows the mouth of Caesar Creek, and the Little Miami River ahead. (Author's photograph)

Behind the scouts and pioneers, Clark's army moved forward in stops and starts. Again and again, the Kentuckians halted while the scouts studied possible ambush sites, or the axemen removed or bridged obstacles. After advancing 14 miles, Clark's army reached Sharon Creek. There, in what is now Sharon Woods Park in Sharonville, the Kentuckians halted at their second Ohio camp.

On August 3, Black Snake's Kispoko warriors and Wryneck's Peckuwes arrived from Peckuwe to reinforce Black Hoof's men. Clark's army advanced another 14 miles to Clark's third Ohio camp, on Turtle Creek southwest of what is now Lebanon.

On August 4, Bird's men and 150 surviving prisoners at last reached Detroit. That day, Clark's men marched to the mouth of Caesar Creek on the Little Miami, and crossed the river 2 miles upstream. They then, after a 12-mile march, halted at Clark's fourth Ohio camp, across the Little Miami from modern Waynesville.

Eighteen miles ahead, messengers had brought to a worried Black Hoof reports on additional reinforcements. Cornstalk's brother Silver Heels was bringing warriors from Mequachake and Wapakoneta. Further up the Mad River, McKee and the great Shawnee war leader Blue Jacket were away. But Buckongahelas, whom many thought the greatest of all Indian commanders, was coming with his Delawares, and so was Simon Girty, with more Shawnees, Wyandots, and Mingos.

They would not, however, arrive in time. Even with Black Snake's and Wryneck's reinforcements, Black Hoof had too few warriors to attack Clark's army, and a defensive battle at Chalawgatha, moreover, would not end like that with Bowman's Kentuckians the year before. Clark's guns would destroy the town's council house and other wooden structures.

Word soon spread that Chalawgatha and its corn would be abandoned. There was anger as the Indians began preparing to leave for Peckuwe, and fear, as hostile eyes turned on terrified young captives like Stephen Ruddell, who would soon become the Shawnee Sinnanatha, and Sarah Loveless, who would live her life as the Wyandot Sohorass.

On August 5, the Kentuckians moved forward more slowly. After marching 9 miles up the east bank of the Little Miami, they halted at Clark's fifth Ohio camp, about 2 miles up Glady Run from present Spring Valley. All day, refugees from Chalawgatha had been arriving at Peckuwe.

By sunrise on August 6, the Kentuckians were moving cautiously up Glady Run. At 2.00pm, they reached Chalawgatha. There they saw fires from its burning council house and smaller structures, and then Indians. "Six Indians," remembered Israel Morrison of Captain John Kennedy's company, "rode from behind the council house and dashed off toward Pickaway."

From the Ohio River to Peckuwe.

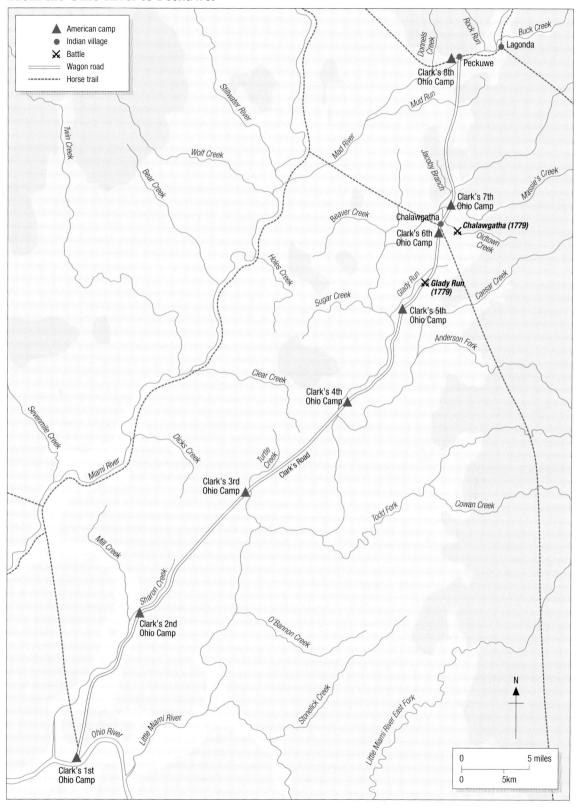

Legend:
- ▲ American camp
- ● Indian village
- ✕ Battle
- Wagon road
- Horse trail

Stillwater River

Twin Creek

Wolf Creek

Bear Creek

Mad River

Donnels Creek

Rock Run

Buck Creek

Lagonda

Clark's 8th Ohio Camp

Peckuwe

Mud Run

Jacoby Branch

Massie's Creek

Beaver Creek

Clark's 7th Ohio Camp

Chalawgatha

Chalawgatha (1779) ✕

Clark's 6th Ohio Camp

Oldtown Creek

Holes Creek

Glady Run

Glady Run (1779) ✕

Caesar Creek

Clark's 5th Ohio Camp

Sugar Creek

Anderson Fork

Clear Creek

Clark's 4th Ohio Camp

Sevenmile Creek

Dicks Creek

Turtle Creek

Clark's Road

Cowan Creek

Miami River

Clark's 3rd Ohio Camp

Todd Fork

Mill Creek

Sharon Creek

O'Bannon Creek

Clark's 2nd Ohio Camp

Stonelick Creek

N

Little Miami River

Ohio River

Little Miami River East Fork

Clark's 1st Ohio Camp

0	5 miles
0	5km

Beside the smoking ruins, the hungry Kentuckians halted at their sixth Ohio camp. The flight of the Indians did not deceive Clark. They were, he later wrote, just "leading us on to their own ground and time of action." His camps now would have more than sentries to guard them. Half his encamped men, Clark ordered, now would remain awake every night.

In the nearby cornfields, ripening ears hung in seemingly endless profusion. "That afternoon," remembered Wilson, "was spent in feasting." Most carried armfuls of corn back to the camp, where they would crack the hard kernels, but some couldn't wait. "There was a brother of John Rice's," Clinkenbeard remembered, "that ate fifteen roasting ears in the field before he cooked any, or came out, so I was told. I did not see it."

On August 7, Silver Heels arrived in Peckuwe with his reinforcements. Now the Indians had 300 warriors, and tomorrow Buckongahelas and Girty would arrive. Then they would have another 150 from Blue Jacket's Town and Wapatomica, Buckongahelas's Town and Zane's Town, Solomon's Town, and Darby's Town.

Since Clark's army had crossed the Ohio, the Shawnee shamans had been searching in the darkness of the future for glimpses of what was to come. Among them was the ancient Assakatoma, who was said to be nearly 100. And the younger Penagashea, who would teach Tecumseh's brother The Prophet the shamanic arts. For days they had studied burnt bones and induced visions. They had at last reached a conclusion. They had seen victory, the shamans announced, in a dawn attack on Clark's encamped army.

Some thought it best to wait for Buckongahelas's and Girty's warriors and then attack on August 9. But most were eager to fight at once. The Indian commanders decided to lead their warriors to a position near the Kentuckians' camp at Chalawgatha, and attack at sunrise on August 8.

Soon painted warriors were dancing around poles, whooping and preparing for battle. At a distance, the turkey feathers in their hair distinguished them as Indians, and on closer view, their gleaming ear and

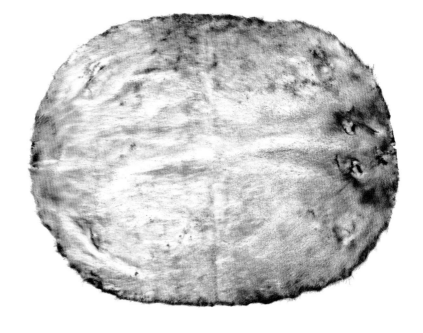

Spirits sometimes appeared in shamans' visions to offer advice. In 1777, an Ojibwe shaman confessed to de Peyster that he had planned to murder the British officer. The spirit of an albino beaver, he said, had told him in a vision to commit the deed. To cleanse his mind, the astute British commander responded, the shaman must track down the beaver and kill it. After the war, de Peyster kept this souvenir of his service on the Ohio River frontier, the wicked beaver's pelt. (King's Regiment Collection, Liverpool Art Museum)

nose rings, and painted faces. But beneath the paint, the faces differed. Some were darker, like those of Black Skin, Muddy Man, and Young Caesar, all adopted black slaves or their descendants. Others were paler, like those of 35-year-old Samuel Saunders, once a Jewish boy in London's East End; 20-year-old Bill Frame, who had been a settler's son on the upper Ohio and would become a famous raider; and 25-year-old Joseph Rogers. Four years after his capture, Clark's cousin was now an adopted Shawnee warrior.

That afternoon, Black Hoof, Black Snake, Wryneck, and Silver Heels led the Indians toward Chalawgatha. After 5 miles, they halted. With a small party of warriors, the Indian commanders then left the trail, and moved south through the woods to inspect the Kentuckians' camp.

Since morning the Kentuckians had been burning the Chalawgatha cornfields, leaving only a section to harvest when they returned. By mid-afternoon, the fields were blackened. Clark finally ordered his officers to form their men into columns to march. That night, he planned, they would camp nearer Peckuwe.

At 4.00pm, the Kentuckians moved north. But after they had advanced only a mile, a terrific thunderstorm struck. Clark then ordered his men to halt and encamp just north of Massie's Creek.

The Indian commanders arrived in the downpour to find the Kentuckians huddled at their seventh Ohio camp. Many of their enemies' firearms, the pleased chiefs foresaw, would be ineffective when they attacked the next morning.

At 7.00pm, the rain ended. The startled Indians then heard a volley of gunfire. Every minute another followed from a different direction. The Kentucky commander, the puzzled Indian chiefs finally realized, had ordered his men to fire and reload their wet rifles.

Clark had told them, Bradford remembered, to "examine their guns and, to be sure that they were in good order, to discharge them in the following manner – one company was to fire, and time given to reload, when a

The appearance today of the site of Clark's seventh Ohio camp, looking south toward a bike trail bridge across Massie's Creek. (Author's photograph)

company at the most remote part of the camp from that which had fired, was to discharge theirs, and so on alternately, until all the guns were fired." "The men," recalled Wilson, "had taken better care of their guns during the rain than Clark had expected, and not over one fourth but went off."

Impressed by Clark's caution, the Indian commanders decided to wait for Buckongahelas' and Girty's reinforcements. The next day, they thought, Clark would camp nearer Peckuwe, and attack the town at dawn on August 9. But the attack on the morning of August 9 would not be by the Kentuckians. Before they moved on August 9, 450 Indians would attack their camp in the battle the shamans apparently had foreseen.

As the Indian party moved back toward Peckuwe in darkness, the rain returned. There was, Ballard remembered, "thunder and lightning and rain nearly all night." "Without tents or any other means of shelter from the rain, which fell in torrents," recalled Bradford, "the men were as wet as if they had been plunged into a stream."

As intermittent flashes illuminated the sodden woods, Clark asked the scout James Guthrie to undertake an unusually dangerous mission. He wanted to know, he told Guthrie, what awaited the Kentuckians at Peckuwe.

THE BATTLE OF PECKUWE

5.00am to 12.00pm

Before the first light of August 8 appeared in the sky at 5.15am, an exhausted Guthrie arrived at the Kentuckians' camp. At Peckuwe, he reported, a three-sided fort overlooked a big village surrounded by many small Indian camps. The place was full of Indians.

Today, Clark thought, they would fight. He ordered his weary, waterlogged men, half of whom had had two sleepless nights, to form in companies and test their rifles again. "All," remembered Ballard, were "reloaded and ready for action."

The Indians, the Kentucky commander thought, were waiting for them to advance to ground where they would be vulnerable to ambush or attack. More men, he concluded, should search for signs of Indians ahead, behind and on the flanks of the army. By the time the sun rose at 5.44am, Whitley

After their defeat in Lord Dunmore's War, the Peckuwe and Kispoko Shawnee had emigrated from their Scioto River towns on the Pickaway Plains to the Mad River, where their adjacent villages usually were called just Peckuwe. The photograph shows the appearance of the site today, as seen from the center of Clark's initial battle line. The triangular fort was on the high ground occupied by the white Hertzler House on the left. Peckuwe was on the lower ground to the right, and Kispoko still further to the right. (Photograph by Chris Crowley)

The Mad River today, looking downstream from the site of the upper ford. (Photograph by Leslie Arendt)

and many others were moving into the woods to join Kenton, Boone, and the other scouts.

Behind them, the sound of falling trees broke the humid silence. "I was pioneer to cut a road for the cannon that day," remembered Clinkenbeard. As the sun rose higher, Oldham led the advance guard forward. Sweat then replaced the rain that had soaked the Kentuckians during the night. There was, remembered Clark, "excessive heat."

After crossing the Little Miami, the Kentuckians moved slowly north. Expecting an attack at any moment, they warily watched the 50ft-high cliffs above them on the river's west bank. At last, after crossing the river's Jacoby Branch, the horses began pulling the guns and wagon up onto higher ground.

After marching through prairie west of modern Yellow Springs, the Kentuckians turned northwest toward Clear Creek. Clark's scouts then reported that they had found in the mud ahead countless moccasin prints left the night before. "The Indians," remembered Israel Morrison, "had come this far to meet Clark's army."

At Peckuwe, many of the warriors were asleep, waiting for Buckongahelas' and Girty's reinforcements to arrive. But the rest of the population, swollen by refugees from Chalawgatha, was busy. Some of the men went hunting south of the Mad River.

Black Hoof, Wryneck, Black Snake, and Silver Heels had left scouts behind to watch Clark's advance. Soon, they hoped, they would learn exactly where Clark's army was halting. They would then begin planning the next morning's attack on the Kentuckians' camp.

Clark's scouts, however, made the task of the watching Indians difficult. Again and again, they saw Clark's men halt, but each time, the Kentuckians resumed their advance. When Clark's men began moving into the rough ground north of Mud Creek, the worried Indian scouts finally concluded that they might be marching all the way to Peckuwe.

The Kentucky scouts, however, made returning directly to Peckuwe by the trail too dangerous. The Indian scouts went back by a longer route. By the time they reached Peckuwe, Indians hunting south of the Mad River were racing to warn the chiefs that Clark's men were approaching. The hunters who had seen the Kentuckians, McKee was told, arrived "at the same time a party of Indians, who had been sent to spy on them, were making their report."

THE BEGINNING OF THE BATTLE, AUGUST 8, 1780, 1.15PM (PP. 52–53)

Suspecting that Indians concealed in the woods ahead might attack his army as it marched up the trail toward Peckuwe, Clark dispatched Colonel James Harrod and 130 men to a position from which they could attack the Indians from behind. When Captain William Oldham's advance guard moved up the trail, the Indians attacked. The scene shows Harrod's men, who are rushing toward the sound of the fighting. Captain Squire Boone (**1**), Daniel Boone's younger brother, is shouting to his men to follow him toward the left. Harrod (**2**) is urging his men forward. An advancing man from Captain Hugh McGary's company, the first to be seen by the Indians, has been shot (**3**). Another of McGary's men (**4**) has taken a firing position behind a tree. Ahead, another (**5**) is battling a Shawnee warrior (**6**) with his rifle. McGary (**7**), who has dropped his firearm, is running forward with a butcher's knife to aid the man. Captain William McAfee (**8**), who will be mortally wounded in the battle, is shouting to his men to follow him toward the right. In the distance, Shawnee warriors (**9**) are attacking Oldham's men. Beyond the scene to their right, Colonel John Floyd's men are racing up the trail to support Oldham's.

Some of the chiefs proposed burning Peckuwe's structures, and occupying a position a few miles beyond the town. With Buckongahelas' and Girty's reinforcements, they argued, the Indians could the next morning attack Clark's army while it was encamped at Peckuwe.

But Black Hoof, Black Snake, and Wryneck were adamant. With Chalawgatha's cornfields gone, the Shawnees could not accept the catastrophic risk that Clark would burn the Peckuwe fields as well. They could not, they said, retreat.

As news of Clark's imminent arrival spread, there was fury. The Shawnee chiefs ordered the recently captured adult males killed. The Indians, Silver Heels remembered, "killed all the male prisoners that were able to desert and give intelligence." Joseph Rogers, who had assimilated well, alone was spared. The Indians, Silver Heels recalled, "had too good an opinion of him."

These alert defenders are guarding a reproduction of the triangular fort near its original site. (Author's photograph)

The chiefs then ordered an evacuation of the women and children. Soon guards were herding Stephen Ruddell, Sarah Loveless, and the other captives to a secure location. With them went Margaret Pauley, who had been captured in 1779 and adopted by the Chalawgatha chief White Bark. "I was taken," she remembered, "with other prisoners, and secreted in the woods within hearing of the firing."

The Indian women and children were sent to another refuge. One protested. He was old enough to fight, 12-year-old Tecumseh said. But the frustrated boy instead was led to safety with his 5-year-old brother Lalawethika, who would win fame as The Prophet.

By then, some of Clark's scouts had reached high ground about 100ft above the Mad River. Before them, a low area of marshy ground extended nearly half a mile toward the river, which curved away, then back, and then away again. The river could be crossed at two fords. To their left, the trail from Chalawgatha reached the lower ford. Far upriver to their right was the upper ford, from which a trail led to Lagonda, a small Shawnee village at the mouth of Buck Creek.

Beyond the lower ford, the trail from Chalawgatha led north about 400 yards to a point where it met another trail. To the left, that trail led west to the Miami River, and on to Peter Loramie's trading post. To the right, it led to the upper ford.

Beyond the trail was a long, high, wooded ridge. Between the river and the ridge the trail passed through gently rising ground. To the far left, beyond the lower ford, woods extended to the ridge. To the right, the ground was prairie as far as the upper ford.

Between the river and the trail, hundreds of acres of cornfields extended for more than a mile. Beyond the trail lay the structures of Peckuwe. Amid the town's many bark-covered wigwams rose two large council houses and about 50 log cabins. On an elevation above the far left of Peckuwe, the Union Jack flew above a blockhouse enclosed by a triangular stockade.

12.00pm to 2.00pm

By noon, Clark's axemen had felled their last tree south of the Mad River. The path to the lower ford, the Kentucky commander was told, now was cleared – and the ford had a rocky bottom. The guns and wagon could cross without a bridge.

After the axemen rejoined their companies, Clark resumed the army's advance. Oldham's 80-man advance guard went forward, Bradford remembered, "in sight of the main army." Behind it on the road went the guns, wagon, and packhorses. To their left and right marched the four columns of Clark's army. Nearly 100 yards to the left of the road, companies from Linn's Regiment occupied the front part of the column, and Harrod's Regiment the rear. In the column to their right, more of Linn's companies were in the front, and some of Logan's in the rear. To their right, beyond the road, Floyd's Regiment marched at the head of the column, and more of Logan's companies behind. On the far right, nearly 100 yards beyond the road, Slaughter's Illinois Regiment companies led the way, and still more of Logan's followed. Behind came the 80-man rearguard.

Ahead, the panicked chiefs at Peckuwe had agreed on a response to Clark's surprise appearance. Outnumbered more than 3:1 by a force with artillery, their only hope of victory lay in delaying the Kentuckians until Buckongahelas' and Girty's reinforcements arrived. They decided to attempt an ambush, which would begin an operation to divert the Kentuckians from the town for several hours.

Clark, they thought, must be led to believe that the Indians were not aware of his advance. He would lead his army across the Mad River at the lower ford. He would continue up the trail toward Peckuwe through prairie, past a large cornfield on the right, and woods on the left. He would halt ahead of the town to move his men from their advancing columns into a battle line.

Then, while the Kentuckians were disorganized, the Indians would attack. Some 225 warriors concealed in the cornfield, prairie, and woods, would assault Clark's rear and flanks. Another 75 from Peckuwe would attack his front. If the ambush failed, the warriors in the cornfield would retreat to Peckuwe.

Those in the prairie and woods would slowly withdraw to the ridge, leading their enemies after them. They would then fall back to a natural defensive position on the ridge. About 600 yards west of the triangular fort, two large oak trees had fallen so that they together formed a rough line of trunk about 50 yards long. When strengthened with additional logs, the trunks would become a nearly invisible breastwork. If the Indians could not hold the breastwork, they would lead the Kentuckians further north, to the East Fork of Donnels Creek. There, they would fight until Buckongahelas' and Girty's warriors arrived.

When Oldham's men reached the lower ford, Clark ordered it to halt while he assessed the situation. The behavior of the Indians was puzzling. Hundreds had advanced to attack his camp on Massie's Creek, but then retreated; and they since had made no attempt to halt his advance.

Clark expected to hear from his scouts that the Indians were fleeing from Peckuwe. But they instead reported that the Indians were there; and, he was told, they seemed unaware that the Kentuckians were near. "The Indians," Sandusky remembered, "appeared calm and composed, walking or standing about in perfect order."

That the Indians would attempt to defend Peckuwe had been too much to hope for. His much larger army, Clark concluded, could be safely dispersed in a rough semicircle around the village, and he could trap the Indians against the Mad River.

The terrain provided five routes of escape. The Indians could flee east from Peckuwe to the upper ford, or northeast into wooded high ground. Logan's regiment would advance across the upper ford to occupy that ground. The Indians also could retreat across the lower ford, west down the river, or north into the woods. The rest of the army would cross at the lower ford and form a line extending west from the river. Harrod's men, on the far left, would block retreat to the north, and meet Logan's to complete the semicircle. Oldham's, Floyd's, Linn's and Slaughter's men, and the rearguard would prevent escape across the lower ford or to the west. Clark, however, did not for a moment believe that the Indians were unaware that his army was across the Mad River. They wanted him to cross at the lower ford and advance up the trail to attack Peckuwe. They probably, he concluded, had concealed warriors to the west of Peckuwe to attack his left flank as he advanced.

Clark immediately dispatched scouts to determine whether the river could be crossed below the lower ford. Nearly 500 yards downstream, they reported, the water was low enough. The Kentucky commander then modified his plan to guard against the ambush he foresaw.

Logan's regiment, reduced to 235 by detachment of men to the rearguard, still would cross at the upper ford, and was to occupy the high wooded ground. Harrod's 130 men, however, would not cross at the lower ford with Oldham's, Floyd's, Linn's, and Slaughter's, and the rearguard. After crossing at the ford further downstream, they would march north to a position in the woods near the Indian trail to Loramie's Trading Post. There they would await the men who had crossed at the lower ford, and advanced up the trail. Harrod's men, at the far left of an initial battle line reaching northeast from the river, then would extend the line around Peckuwe to meet Logan's.

The change anticipated an Indian plan to attack the Kentuckians as they moved up the trail from the lower ford. Harrod's men, Clark hoped, might reach their position undetected. If they did, and the Indians attacked, the warriors would themselves be assaulted from behind by Harrod's men.

Soon Kenton was leading Logan's men northeast toward the upper ford. But he found their route blocked by flooded low ground. Kenton tried one path, and then another, in growing frustration. The Kentuckians, Thomas remembered, "got entangled in the swamp."

Harrod's men found the path easier. Sandusky, who was with his father in Harrod's Regiment, remembered the reaction when Clark's orders were

James Harrod, aged 34 in 1780, had led a company in Andrew Lewis's army during Lord Dunmore's War. In 1792, he would be killed by an unknown assailant while searching for a silver mine reportedly found by the early explorer Jonathan Swift. The photograph shows reconstructed Fort Harrod at Old Fort Harrod State Park in Harrodsburg. (Graphic Enterprises)

PECKUWE, AUGUST 8, 1780: THE AMERICAN ATTACK

Shown here are the events that took place at Peckuwe between 12.00pm and 2.00pm.

Note: gridlines are shown at intervals of 500m (0.31 miles)

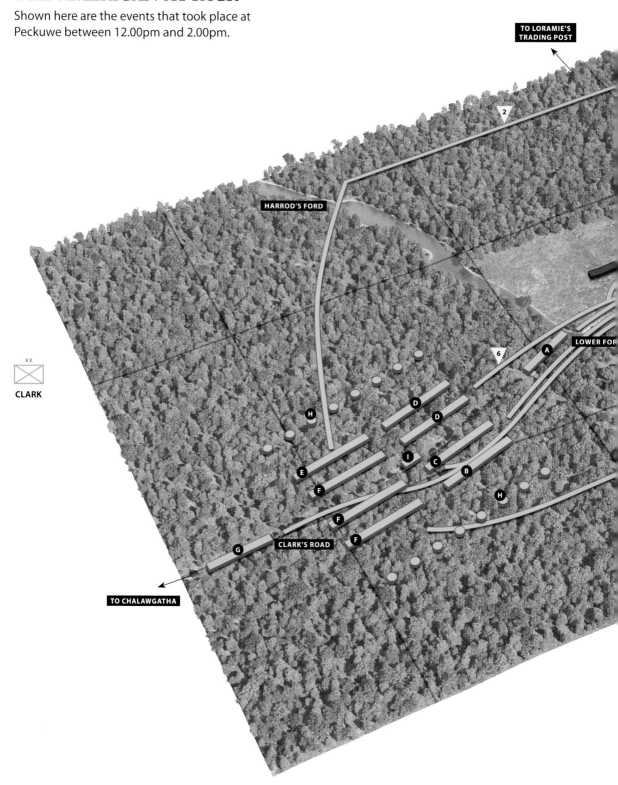

TO LORAMIE'S TRADING POST

HARROD'S FORD

CLARK

LOWER FOR

CLARK'S ROAD

TO CHALAWGATHA

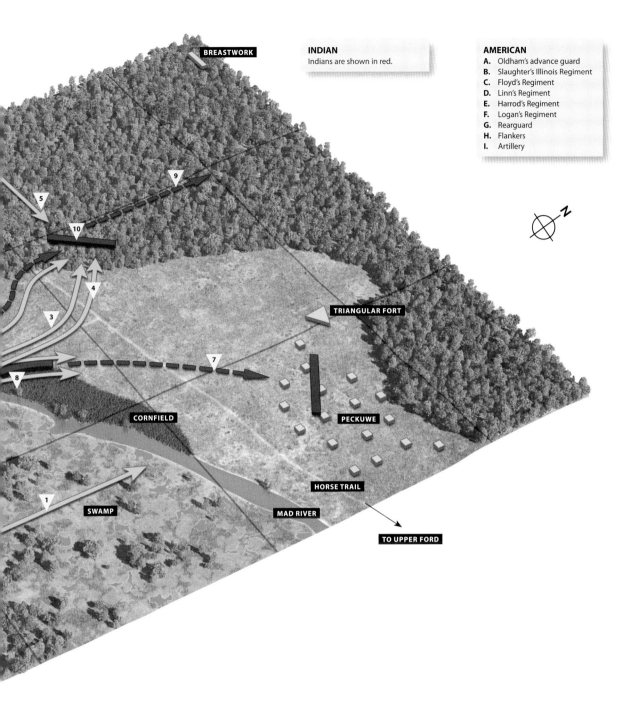

BREASTWORK

INDIAN
Indians are shown in red.

AMERICAN
A. Oldham's advance guard
B. Slaughter's Illinois Regiment
C. Floyd's Regiment
D. Linn's Regiment
E. Harrod's Regiment
F. Logan's Regiment
G. Rearguard
H. Flankers
I. Artillery

TRIANGULAR FORT

CORNFIELD

PECKUWE

HORSE TRAIL

SWAMP

MAD RIVER

TO UPPER FORD

EVENTS

1. Logan's Regiment advances toward the upper ford into swampy ground.

2. Harrod's Regiment crosses the Mad River at Harrod's Ford and advances to assigned position.

3. Oldham's advance guard crosses the Mad River at the lower ford and is attacked as it advances to its assigned position in the woods.

4. Floyd's Regiment advances to support Oldham's advance guard.

5. Harrod's Regiment attacks Indians from the rear.

6. Linn's Regiment crosses the river and drives the Indians from the prairie and cornfield.

7. Indians in the prairie and cornfield retreat.

8. Slaughter's Illinois Regiment, reargard, and Artillery cross the river and begin forming Clark's initial battle line.

9. Indians in the woods retreat to the ridge.

10. Men in Oldham's, Floyd's, Harrod's, and Linn's units halt in the woods and form a battle line.

As Logan's men moved toward the upper ford, Kenton remembered, they could see across the Mad River "fields of corn in every heart of the creek." The photograph, taken about 500 yards below the upper ford, shows corn growing now across the river, in one of the fields Kenton saw. (Author's photograph)

announced. "My father," he recalled, "was mightily pleased when he heard the order. He didn't want to go where those Indians were so composed." He thought, Sandusky recalled, "that in the point in the woods they would be pleasantly situated."

As Harrod's men advanced, Logan's found their route blocked by flooded low ground. Kenton tried one path, and then another, in growing frustration. The Kentuckians, Thomas remembered, "got entangled in the swamp."

The Kentucky commander, who had heard no gunfire from the directions in which Logan's and Harrod's men had advanced, judged that they had encountered no opposition. When he finally concluded that they must be nearing their assigned positions, he ordered Oldham to lead the advance guard across the lower ford and up the trail. He then, before reaching Peckuwe, was to lead his men left into the woods, find Harrod's men, and halt to their right. Floyd's and Linn's men, who would follow, would form to Oldham's right toward the river. Slaughter's men then would form to the left of the river, and the rearguard would complete the line between Linn's men and Slaughter's.

The advance guard crossed, Wilson remembered, through water "knee deep." Oldham's men then marched up the trail. Ahead and to their left the prairie grass was as high as 6ft. "To the right and along the stream, and just before reaching the wood," Wilson recalled, "was a large cornfield. Along the margin of this field, and parallel with the river, ran a pole fence."

The Indians in the prairie and cornfield watched silently as Oldham's men passed on the trail. The warriors in the woods also observed their approach. But the Indians behind the trees received a surprise. Instead of following the trail toward Peckuwe, the Kentuckians turned left and began moving into the woods directly toward them.

Ballard remembered how the battle began. The advance guard, he recalled, "encountered ten Indians in the woodland. Two of Oldham's men were shot down at the onset. The others rushed up and drove the Indians from their sheltered position."

The warriors in the woods then received an even greater surprise. Harrod's men, who had reached their position, heard the fire, and began moving toward the fighting. Soon they reached the rear of the Indians battling Oldham's men. "The first they knew," Sandusky recalled, "a gun fired and killed one man. The action was then brought on." "A severe battle," remembered Robert McAfee, "now commenced, and a running tree fire was kept up."

As Floyd's men began to ford the river, scattered shots came at them from the prairie

The battle began in the then wooded area to the right of and beyond the Davidson Interpretative Center, the structure in the distance. (Photograph by Leslie Arendt)

on the opposite bank. Worried about Oldham's isolated men, apparently under heavy fire ahead, Clark ordered Floyd to ignore the shots, cross the river, and race up the trail to support them. As balls flew past, Floyd's men rushed forward toward the woods. More shots came as they passed the cornfield. The Indians there, Wilson remembered, "fired upon the troops but fifty yards as they ran along the prairie."

Clark then ordered Linn to advance. But they were not to race up the trail. They were instead to drive the Indians from the prairie and cornfield. When Linn's men moved into the ford, the warriors in the prairie again opened fire, but the Kentuckians splashed forward. Soon Abraham Whitaker of Captain Michael Humble's company was scurrying up the bank. A year before, his shot had killed Black Fish at Chalawgatha. "He was," remembered Ballard, "a very noted marksman and a great Indian fighter. He could outrun any Indians, and he with a rifle in each hand."

Soon after Floyd returned from the campaign, his wife produced a son, whom they named for the Kentucky commander. Twenty-one years later, George Rogers Clark Floyd would play an important role at Tippecanoe. The 1779 springhouse at Floyd's Station survives in what is now St Matthews, KY. (The Filson Historical Society; photograph by James Holmberg)

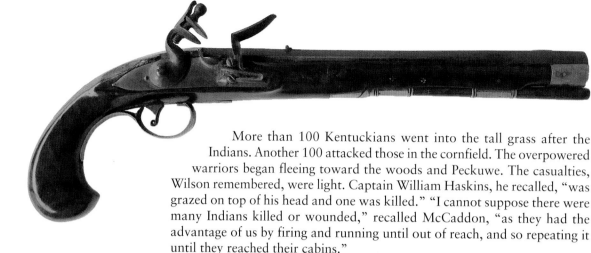

Forty-six in 1780, Linn had been wounded leading a company at Wakatomica. He had then, before emigrating to Kentucky, saved his company of upper Ohio militiamen by refusing to follow the path into ambush at McMechen's Narrows. This pistol belonged to Linn. (Photograph by Mel Hankla)

More than 100 Kentuckians went into the tall grass after the Indians. Another 100 attacked those in the cornfield. The overpowered warriors began fleeing toward the woods and Peckuwe. The casualties, Wilson remembered, were light. Captain William Haskins, he recalled, "was grazed on top of his head and one was killed." "I cannot suppose there were many Indians killed or wounded," recalled McCaddon, "as they had the advantage of us by firing and running until out of reach, and so repeating it until they reached their cabins."

Clark then ordered the rest of his army across the river. Slaughter's Illinois Regiment companies marched to their position immediately to the left of the river, where, about 400 yards from Peckuwe, they formed the far right of Clark's battle line. The guns, wagon, and packhorses followed. The rearguard advanced to a position to Slaughter's left. To their left, fighting raged in the woods.

Finally, the Indians there fled back to the ridge. They "broke and run 200 yards," Wilson remembered, "and again rallied and formed on a hill covered with timber." "The Indians," recalled Sandusky, "possessed a ground full of ridges, about a gun shot off. They fired and then run till they got another opportunity to fire."

Clark's concealed deployment of Harrod's men, and his order to Oldham to leave the trail, had disrupted the Indians' planned ambush. But in the woods there was chaos. Captain Lewis Hickman of Linn's Regiment, who had run into the trees ahead of his men, had vanished. Oldham's, Harrod's, Floyd's, and Linn's men were scattered and intermingled.

All were eager to charge up the ridge after their foes. But the cautious Kentucky commander went into the woods to stop them. Clark, Wilson remembered "halted the troops in the woods for a few minutes, and got the men in order, who had in crossing the river and running through the prairie become disarranged."

2.00pm to 5.30pm

Although many of the Kentuckians in the woods were no longer in their original companies, they soon formed the left wing of a battle line that extended 800 yards to the river. At the far left were Oldham's 80 men, Harrod's 130, and Floyd's 120. In the center were Linn's 235. To their right were the 80 men in the rearguard, and then Slaughter's 70, their flank protected by the river. Behind them were the artillerymen, guns, wagon, and horses. Facing them were about 150 Indians on the wooded ridge, and another 150 in Peckuwe.

Clark then ordered his left wing and center to advance. Oldham's, Harrod's, and Floyd's 330 men were to turn the right flank of the Indians on the ridge. They then were to wheel clockwise, herding the warriors back toward Peckuwe until Oldham's men at the far left finally reached Logan's.

Linn's men were to occupy the low ground to the southwest, and the area of the ridge to the west, of the triangular fort.

Clark, Wilson recalled, "ordered the men in attacking the Indians to press upon them, and not suffer them to fire twice behind the same tree." The ascent of the ridge, remembered Charles Kennedy of Captain Peter Sturgis's company, was "hard fought." "Pretty much all the men of the left wing were engaged," Ballard recalled.

The Kentuckians, Wilson remembered, "marched on up the elevation and attacked the Indians, took trees, and pressed warmly on them." The fighting extended continually to the west as the Indians on the ridge tried to outflank the Kentuckians' left, and the Kentuckians the Indians' right. From time to time, warriors made it around to the Kentuckians' rear. But they were few and scattered. "These," Wilson recalled, "would have to be met by simply wheeling upon, and a fire or two would drive them off."

Excited by the attack, the rearguard and Slaughter's companies went forward as well. Soon balls were flying at them. "While we went through that prairie," Clinkenbeard remembered, "the Indians fired upon us from their cabins. Could see them come out of their cabins as unconcerned as I would go out of my door, and shoot. Held their guns too high. Could hear them 'biz,' 'biz' over us."

But Clark ordered his right wing to halt before it reached the effective range of musket fire from Peckuwe. "The party I had joined," remembered Thomas, "was about entering the town with great impetuosity when General Clark sent orders for us to stop, as the Indians were making port holes in their cabins, and we should be in great danger."

As Oldham's, Harrod's, and Floyd's men advanced, the Shawnee warriors fell back to their concealed breastwork. "The Indians," Wilson recalled, "finally retreated a hundred yards off, to a couple of large oak trees which lay prostrate in a parallel line. On top of these were placed chunks and poles stretched along lengthwise on their top forming a very good breastwork with something like portholes between the poles and main body of the tree. Here some 50 Indians posted themselves undiscovered to fire upon the advancing whites."

Captain Joseph McMurtry of Harrod's Regiment was the first to come in sight. McMurtry, Wilson remembered, "was within 30 steps of the Indian breastwork, without knowing the Indians were there." When he halted to reload his rifle, "the Indians behind the oak trees all fired at the same time."

The appearance today of the area of the wooded ridge taken by Floyd's and Harrod's men. (Photograph by Tom Ratterman)

THE AMERICAN ATTACK ON THE RIDGE, AUGUST 8, 1780, 2.15PM (PP. 64–65)

After driving the Indians from the woods to the west of Peckuwe, Oldham's, Harrod's, and Floyd's 330 Kentuckians formed a line facing the ridge west of the triangular fort. They then charged up the ridge, driving back the 150 Shawnee warriors defending it. Now they are advancing north, fighting from tree to tree. On the far left, the men in Captain William Oldham's advance guard are trying to move beyond the Shawnees' far right, hoping to turn the Indians' flank and force them back toward Peckuwe. The scene shows the extreme left of Oldham's line. An alarmed Daniel Boone (1) has detected movement in the woods behind the Kentuckians. Concerned that it might be by Indians, he has alerted Bland Ballard, who is second in command of Oldham's unit. Ballard (2) is closely studying the foreground ahead of the scene. Two Kentuckians (3) and (4) are hurrying further to the left. Kentuckians to their right are fighting the Indians. One (5) is reloading his rifle. Another (6) is firing his rifle at an Indian ahead. Oldham (7) is shouting to men to his right beyond the scene to hurry on toward the left. A Shawnee warrior (8) has fired his musket at a Kentuckian. Other Shawnees (9) are rushing to extend the right flank of the Indian line.

As one ball severed the Kentucky captain's right forefinger, another passed through his powder horn and entered his chest. But the second ball, flattened by McMurtry's powder horn, made only a superficial wound. None of the other Indian balls reached a Kentucky target. "But a single man was hurt," Wilson remembered, "and that was Captain McMurtry."

The Indians, who had lost their opportunity to surprise the Kentuckians by their premature fire, now would be attacked on their flanks. To avoid being surrounded, they fell back 400 yards to the north. The retreating Indians offered heavy resistance. Ballard was shot, he recalled, "in his left thigh while treed." He had just "shot down one Indian, and was trying to get off another shot."

Wilson, who saw three Indians hiding in bushes, killed one wearing a cocked hat that the Kentuckian coveted. As he searched for his prize, captains Robert Elliston and William McAfee led several men to the scene. The second Indian, Robert McAfee recalled, mortally wounded his uncle by a shot "through the breast." James McBride of Elliston's company, Wilson remembered, "discovering the Indian by the smoke of his gun, fired at him and killed him on the spot, which ended his exultation." Another ball felled the third Indian.

Eight years after the battle, Ballard would become a legendary figure. Returning to his cabin on March 1, 1788, he saw at a distance Indians massacring the members of his family. Unable to save them, he one by one killed six of the raiders with his rifle. Ballard would lead companies at Fallen Timbers in 1794, and at the January 18 and 22, 1813 battles of the River Raisin during the War of 1812. At the second battle of the River Raisin, he would be struck by a ball exactly where he had been hit at Peckuwe 33 years before. This c.1850 daguerreotype is of a portrait of the great frontiersman by an unknown artist. (Wisconsin Historical Society, WHS 109566)

Slaughter's men, the rearguard, and Linn's Regiment, which had taken the ground it had charged, now were in their assigned positions. Logan, Clark hoped, also was in his. But Oldham's, Harrod's, and Floyd's men were battling Indians on the left in fighting that was moving ever further away. The men on his far left, Linn finally reported, had lost contact with those on Floyd's far right.

Clark's army now was divided into three parts that could not communicate. Oldham's, Harrod's, and Floyd's 330 men soon were more than a mile north of Clark's line of 405. Logan's 235 had abandoned hope of advancing through the swamp. They now were moving south toward higher ground, further from Clark with every step.

The artillery, Lieutenant Richard Harrison reported, was ready for action. But the 6lb gun could not be elevated high enough to fire on the triangular fort. The piece, Clark concluded, would have to be moved to the high ground that Linn had occupied. Soon axemen began cutting through the woods a course toward the gun's new firing position.

To signal his location to his distant commanders, Clark decided to open fire with his guns. The Kentuckian, who did not want the Indians dispersed, chose ammunition that would herd them into the triangular fort and other wooden structures. The Kentuckians' rifle balls, the Indians knew, had little

PECKUWE, AUGUST 8, 1780: THE INDIAN DEFENSE

Shown here are the events at Peckuwe between 2.00pm and 5.30pm.

Note: gridlines are shown at intervals of 1km (0.62 miles)

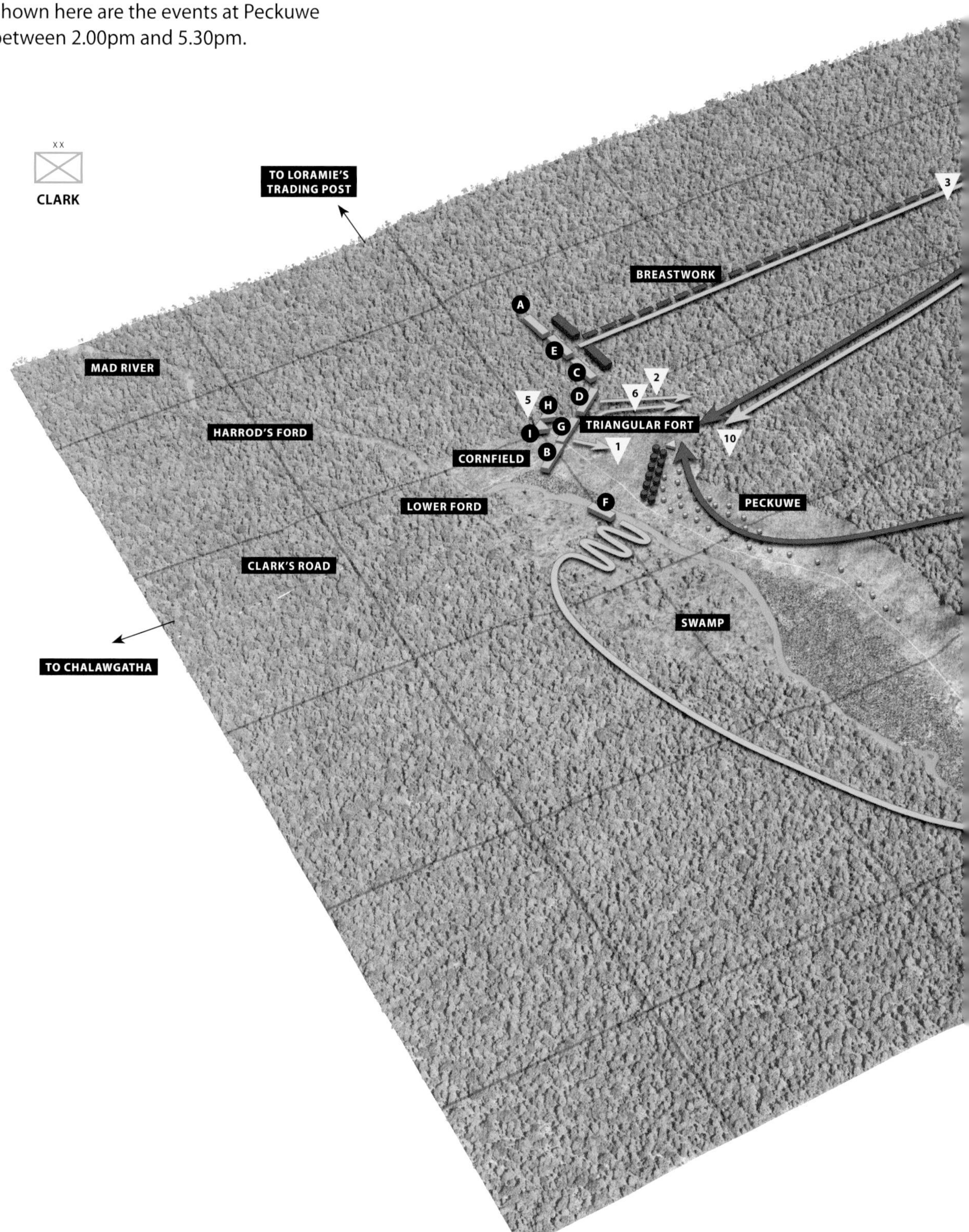

XX
CLARK
TO LORAMIE'S TRADING POST
BREASTWORK
MAD RIVER
HARROD'S FORD
TRIANGULAR FORT
CORNFIELD
LOWER FORD
PECKUWE
CLARK'S ROAD
SWAMP
TO CHALAWGATHA
A
B
C
D
E
F
G
H
I
1
2
3
5
6
10

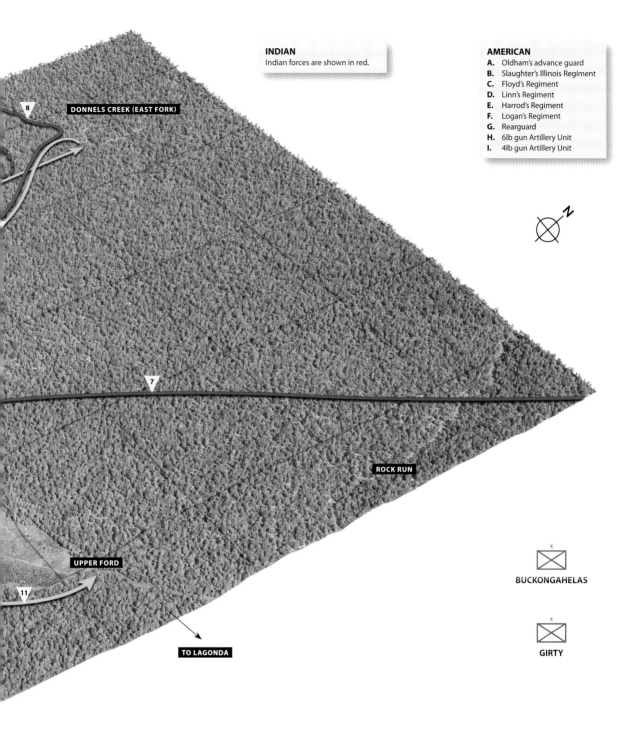

INDIAN
Indian forces are shown in red.

AMERICAN
A. Oldham's advance guard
B. Slaughter's Illinois Regiment
C. Floyd's Regiment
D. Linn's Regiment
E. Harrod's Regiment
F. Logan's Regiment
G. Rearguard
H. 6lb gun Artillery Unit
I. 4lb gun Artillery Unit

DONNELS CREEK (EAST FORK)

ROCK RUN

UPPER FORD

TO LAGONDA

BUCKONGAHELAS

GIRTY

EVENTS

1. Illinois Regiment, rearguard, and Artillery advance toward Peckuwe and halt beyond musket range.

2. Linn's Regiment advances to occupy high ground overlooking the triangular fort.

3. Advance guard, Harrod's Regiment, and Floyd's Regiment advance, capture Indian breastwork, and pursue Indians to East Fork of Donnels Creek.

4. Indians retreat to East Fork of Donnels Creek and disperse.

5. Clark's guns fire on Peckuwe with grapeshot.

6. Clark moves 6lb gun to new position overlooking the triangular fort.

7. Buckongahelas' and Girty's Indian reinforcements arrive.

8. Indians reassemble at East Fork of Donnels Creek and disclose their force to Advance guard, Harrod's Regiment, and Floyd's Regiment.

9. Advance guard, Harrod's Regiment, and Floyd's Regiment pursue fleeing Indians to high ground above Peckuwe.

10. Joined by their reinforcements, the Indians fail to drive the advance guard, Harrod's Regiment, and Floyd's Regiment from the high ground above Peckuwe and retreat to the triangular fort.

11. Logan's men finally reach the Upper Ford, but cannot cross, and move upstream.

effect beyond 300 yards. But these balls, they would learn, would hit any man not behind a tree trunk or log at twice that distance, and leave in him a massive hole.

Clark ordered Harrison to load his guns with grapeshot. "We just had them filled with grape shot and fired at them," Clinkenbeard remembered. "A discharge of grape shot," recalled Thomas, "scattered the materials of their frail dwellings in every direction." Warriors in wigwams and lean-tos, and behind sheds, fences, and bushes, fled from their concealed locations to safety behind log walls.

After Clark ceased the firing, word arrived in Peckuwe that Buckongahelas, Girty, and 150 warriors were at last nearing the town. Soon Buckongahelas and Girty were reviewing the situation with Black Hoof and the other chiefs. The great Delaware was not optimistic. The outnumbered Indians, Buckongahelas remembered, "were badly armed, had few guns and bad powder. The Americans were well armed with rifles and had the best of powder." As the chiefs debated possible courses of action, Black Hoof sent messengers to retrieve the warriors who had led the left wing of Clark's army so far to the north.

This brass plate, found during a 2016 Wright State University archaeological excavation at the battlefield, decorated the butt of an Indian's British trade musket. (Photograph courtesy of Professor Lance Greene)

After battling Oldham's, Floyd's, and Harrod's men for two hours, the Indian commanders had finally ordered their warriors to disperse and hide near the East Fork of Donnels Creek. Soon the Kentuckians could no longer find targets, and behind them, Clark's guns had fallen silent. "They lost sight of the Indians entirely," remembered McAfee, "and, not hearing anything of the other portion of the army, they collected together and marched back towards the river above the town."

But Oldham's, Harrod's, and Floyd's men soon halted. Uncertain about the best route back to the rest of the army, they stopped on high ground overlooking the East Fork of Donnels Creek. There, McAfee recalled, they "sat down to listen for the balance of the army, but all was silence for near half an hour."

While the Kentuckians listened, Black Hoof's messengers finally found the Indian commanders who had dispersed their warriors. To summon their men, the Indian chiefs began whooping loudly. A growing body of warriors then began moving along the East Fork of Donnels Creek. "Suddenly," McAfee remembered, "a body of Indians came down the bottom below them and commenced tremendous war whoop yelling. The white troops immediately rushed down upon them, and each party taking tree a heavy fire commenced."

"The enemy," Ballard recalled, "seemed to be in for their town as they fought retreating." They were "driven from tree to tree, and stand to stand," Wilson remembered. "When the whites reached to top one ridge," he recalled, "the Indians were ascending another." The retreating Indians finally halted on the last ridge, which overlooked the triangular fort from the north.

As the retreating Indians fought to hold the ridge above Peckuwe, many of Buckongahelas' and Girty's warriors rushed to join them. "When the Indians reached the high ground above the bottom where their town was located," McAfee recalled, "they formed in line of battle and took trees. Here the battle really commenced as the Indians in the fort united with their brethren."

Linn's men, in contact again with Oldham's, Harrod's, and Floyd's, joined the battle too. The fire of more than 500 rifles was too much for the warriors. "After the battle had continued for some time," McAfee remembered, "and several had been killed on both sides, the Indians ran down the hill into their fort and cabins." They "took shelter in their blockhouse," Ballard recalled, "stockaded in." The Indians, Clark remembered, "at last took shelter in their strongholds and woods adjacent, when the firing ceased for about half an hour, while preparations were made for dislodging them."

If Logan's Regiment was in its position, Clark thought, his army soon would be ready to attack the Indians trapped at Peckuwe. Logan's men, however, were still south of the Mad River. They had reached the upper ford. There, remembered Peter Adams of Captain William Hays' company, "In the prairie over the river, the Indians fired on Logan's party."

But the water at the upper ford had proved too deep to cross. Now Kenton was leading them further upstream, searching for a place where the river could be forded. But every place the river was fordable, he found beyond the opposite bank almost vertical cliffs.

5.30pm to 8.00pm

The Indian commanders had at last agreed on a plan to defend Peckuwe. Without the 6lb gun, they had concluded, Clark could not reduce Peckuwe's wooden strongholds. They therefore must capture the piece. About 200

The appearance today of the high ground from which Clark fired his 6lb gun, as seen from the site of the triangular fort. (Photograph by Harmony Arendt)

THE INDIAN ATTACK ON THE AMERICAN 6LB GUN, AUGUST 8, 1780, 6.30PM (PP. 72–73)

Indians attacked Clark's 6lb gun from the rear, and then from the front, but instead of surprising and overpowering the defenders, the Indians found them already formed into a hollow square awaiting the attack. After incurring unexpectedly large casualties, the Indians who had attacked from the rear now are engaged in a fight in which they have no advantage, with enemies whose flanks cannot be turned. The sound of gunfire in the distance, heavy when the Indians were attacking the front of the hollow square, now is diminishing. The scene shows the center of the line of Indians behind the rear of the hollow square after the failure of their initial assault. A wounded Shawnee warrior (1), his arm bound with lichens and bog moss to prevent infection, is resting

against a tree trunk. Another warrior (2) is firing his musket; a dead warrior (3) can be seen just ahead of him. As a wounded warrior (4) crawls back to cover, a crouching friend (5) is aiding him. The absence of a right ear, lost six years earlier at the Battle of Point Pleasant, distinguishes the celebrated Delaware war chief Buckongahelas (6), who is conferring with another commander, the adopted Mingo Simon Girty (7). They agree that the operation, which was premised upon surprising the Kentuckians, now should be halted; that the battle should be ended; and that their warriors should leave Peckuwe. Ahead, a Kentuckian (8) has fired his musket at the wounded Shawnee and his friend. The location of other Kentuckians is revealed by smoke from their gunfire (9).

This reproduction 6lb gun has fired a 6lb ball at the National Muzzle Loading Rifle Association range in Friendship, IN. Jim Campbell, commander of the 1st Mad River Light Artillery Company, is pointing toward the target, which the ball has hit at a distance of 75 yards. (Courtesy of the 1st Mad River Light Artillery Company)

warriors would attack from behind the gun. When they opened fire, another 200 would charge up from the triangular fort.

By then Clark had formed his men into their final battle line. On the far right, Slaughter's companies, the rearguard, and the 4lb gun were in the prairie southwest of Peckuwe. Linn's men extended up onto the high ground overlooking the triangular fort from the northwest, where the 6lb gun was now positioned. Floyd's and Harrod's were on the high ground north of the fort. Oldham's, at the far left, were further east.

As Oldham occupied his position, the Indians who would attack the 6lb gun from the rear, probably led by Buckongahelas and Girty, left the fort by a secret exit and began moving beyond the Kentuckians' far left. As they crept forward, Oldham dispatched men further east to find Logan's regiment.

They had not found Logan, Oldham's men reported, but they had seen a large party of warriors moving around the Kentuckians toward Oldham's rear. When Oldham reported the movement to Clark, the Kentucky commander ordered deployment of units to guard against attack from the rear. The Indians, remembered McCaddon, "sallied around to our left, apparently with the intention of attacking us in the rear. In order to prevent which, a company was ordered back, of which I was one."

The Indians behind them, a puzzled Clark reasoned, must be moving to attack a particular point in his line. Their target, he suddenly realized, must be the 6lb gun. He instantly ordered a redeployment. Two hundred men from Linn's and Floyd's regiments hastily formed a guard surrounding the piece. "The men," Wilson remembered, "were formed on an elevation above the fort into a hollow square."

Wherever Logan might be, Clark was unwilling to delay his attack any further. He ordered the gun crew in the hollow square to open fire. A 6lb ball struck the triangular fort's blockhouse. "The first fire," Ballard remembered, "made the bark fly right merrily." The second "shattered the upper part of the building." "The cannon," Wilson recalled, "was fired a dozen or 15 times from the hollow square, the balls shivering the stockade wherever they struck."

As the walls around them threatened to collapse, the Indian commanders quickly improvised a distraction to halt the bombardment until Buckongahelas' and Girty's Indians had reached their position. The Indians,

Seven years after the battle, Whitley would begin building the first brick house in Kentucky on an estate that contained Kentucky's first racetrack. There he introduced the American custom of counterclockwise horse racing. This portrait of the great frontiersman by an unknown artist hangs in the house, now a museum. (Graphic Enterprises)

Wilson remembered, "opened the only gate in the fort, which fronted Clark." As the astonished Kentuckians watched, they then "marched out and took position on the flat below, and formed into a single line."

"It was," Wilson recalled, "a novel movement." The Kentucky commander, he remembered, "ordered the cannon to cease firing, thinking they had got tired of fighting and were about to propose to treat." As a white flag rose above the Kentuckians, Clark waited for the approach of Indian emissaries.

"A few minutes," Wilson recollected, "dispelled this illusion." The Indians standing in silent order finally heard the signal for which they were waiting. "A heavy fire upon the rear," Wilson recalled, "opened from the woods. This was briskly returned." Then, he recalled, "the Indians on the flat came running in line and fired when within gunshot."

As scattered Indian fire whizzed past, Wilson recalled, Clark gave "strict orders for the men to reserve theirs until the Indians should come close." One of the Kentuckians, he remembered, "Hollered 'Let them come near enough that we can singe their eyebrows.'"

In the rear, where many of Harrod's and Linn's nearby men joined the defense, there were too many rifles for the attackers. "The Indians in the rear," Wilson remembered, "protected by trees, and so were Clark's party, stood about 4 rounds before they scampered to the woods."

Ahead of the square, the Indians swarmed up the slope toward the hollow square. Some found cover behind trees, others surged forward with abandon. "When within forty steps," Wilson recalled, the Kentuckians "showered a volley upon the Indians, which mowed them down terribly and which checked their advancing." A second fire "caused them to retreat."

"Some of Clark's men were shooting at some of the wounded Indians crawling off," Wilson recollected, when a cry came "from behind a stump." "I'm a Virginian," shouted a wounded warrior. He then asked to see Clark.

Beneath the war paint, the Kentucky commander sadly recognized Joseph Rogers, who was dying. "Among the rest we killed an own cousin of General Clark's," remembered Whitley. "He had been a prisoner with the Indians and lived several hours after he was shot."

About three-quarters of a mile beyond the upper ford, Kenton finally found at the mouth of Rock Run a place where Logan's men could cross the river. There the small stream had cut through the cliffs a path to the high wooded ground assigned as their position. The water there, Adams remembered, was "waist deep."

As Logan's men at last moved back toward Peckuwe, Clark ordered his 6lb gun to resume fire. Then he directed his men to advance. The Kentuckians encountered fierce resistance. Captain John Morrison, his daughter remembered, "got shot in the ear in the fight," and was "extremely hurt." The Indians, he told her, "contested by inches, till we got so close the powder flashed in their faces. They stood," he said, "until they were powder burnt."

The Indians found no refuge in the triangular fort. The 6lb gun, Wilson remembered, "played upon the fort 4 or 5 shots." As the walls of the stronghold collapsed around them, Ballard recalled, "the Indians fled from it, not all at once, but a few at a time." "The men," Wilson recalled, "then rushed to the fort."

The retreating Indians sought cover in Peckuwe's log council houses and cabins. "Many of them," Ballard recalled, "took positions in the cabins nearby, and as they ran from these Clark's men would shoot at them." There were, Wilson remembered, "four or five Indians in a cabin below the fort shooting at the men." John Lee and Henry Banta of Captain Hardy Hill's company, he recalled, "upon the side hill, saw this Indian party. Lee fired and while reloading, one of the Indians returned the fire from the cabin and shot the top of Lee's ramrod off as he had it partly rammed down."

After reducing the triangular fort, Clark redirected the big gun's fire toward Peckuwe. Its first ball hit the cabin from which fire had come against Lee. "The cannon," Wilson remembered, "fired a single shot. Passed through. The Indians could not stand thusly and scampered off."

The appearance today of the site where Logan's men finally crossed the Mad River. The mouth of Rock Run is on the right. (Photograph by Leslie Arendt)

PECKUWE, AUGUST 8, 1780: THE FINAL AMERICAN ADVANCE

Shown here are the events at Peckuwe between 5.30pm and 8.00pm.

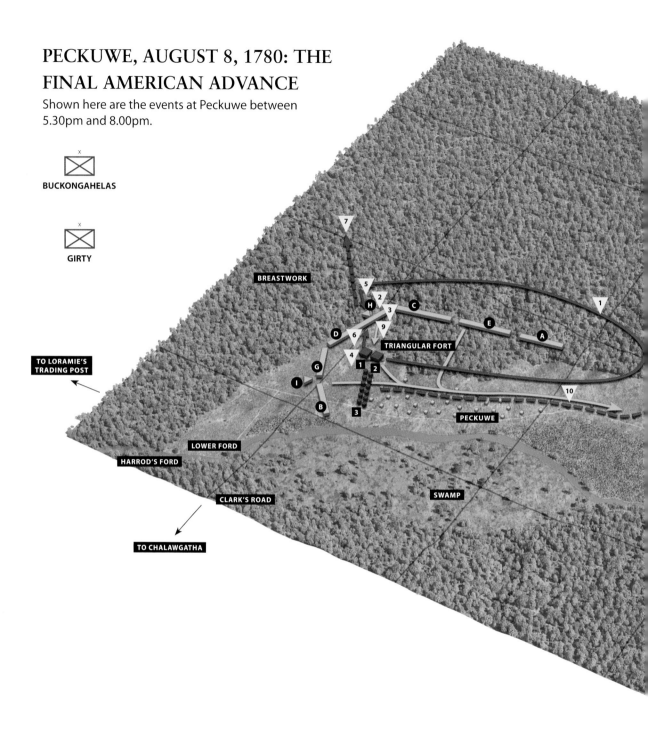

BUCKONGAHELAS

GIRTY

BREASTWORK

TRIANGULAR FORT

TO LORAMIE'S TRADING POST

PECKUWE

LOWER FORD

HARROD'S FORD

CLARK'S ROAD

TO CHALAWGATHA

SWAMP

EVENTS

1. Girty's Indians move around Kentucky left to attack 6lb gun from the rear.
2. Clark deploys companies from Linn's and Floyd's regiments into a hollow square to protect the 6lb gun.
3. The 6lb gun begins bombardment of Triangular Fort.
4. Indians form in line ahead of the fort to halt bombardment.
5. Girty's Indians attack hollow square from rear.
6. Indians attack hollow square from front.
7. Girty's Indians retreat and disperse.
8. Logan's men ford Mad River and begin climbing to high ground.
9. Kentuckians drive Indians back and occupy Triangular Fort.
10. Kentuckians attack Peckuwe.
11. Indians flee from Peckuwe.
12. Logan advances toward Peckuwe too late to block Indian flight.

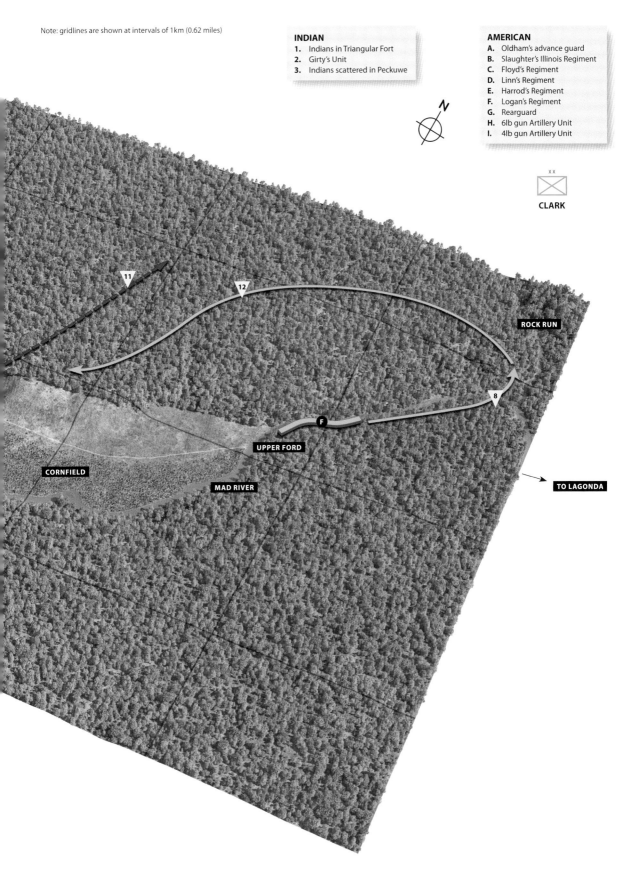

Note: gridlines are shown at intervals of 1km (0.62 miles)

INDIAN
1. Indians in Triangular Fort
2. Girty's Unit
3. Indians scattered in Peckuwe

AMERICAN
A. Oldham's advance guard
B. Slaughter's Illinois Regiment
C. Floyd's Regiment
D. Linn's Regiment
E. Harrod's Regiment
F. Logan's Regiment
G. Rearguard
H. 6lb gun Artillery Unit
I. 4lb gun Artillery Unit

x x
CLARK

ROCK RUN

UPPER FORD

CORNFIELD

MAD RIVER

TO LAGONDA

Clark had anticipated the 18th-century frontier version of urban combat that followed. The balls of the 6lb gun would render the Indians' wooden strongholds deathtraps. "A few shots," remembered Bradford, "dislodged the Indians that were in them." His grapeshot and rifle balls would make the Indians' paths to safety killing fields for those who did not flee quickly. "The Indians," Thomas recalled, "poured out of their cabins in great consternation."

"Our party, and those on the bank," Thomas recalled, "rushed into the village." But the Kentucky commander halted the reckless advance. He ordered his men to advance cautiously as Peckuwe's structures were reduced. "The greatest loss on both sides," Wilson remembered, "was in the action in the town." There, recalled Ballard, "there was much sign of blood." "The firing kept up," McAfee remembered, "until after sun down."

As darkness approached, the Indians vanished. When Logan's men at last reached their assigned position, they were too late to block the Indians' line of escape. In the last dim light of the day, Adams remembered, "they found the Indians just retreating."

After 8.00pm

When the last light left the sky at 8.10pm, Clark ordered his men to encamp. But even in victory, the Kentucky commander remained wary. That night, Wilson remembered, "Nearly one half were on duty. No countersign given, with orders to shoot at every noise or suspicious object." "I reckon that there were three companies of us that went out about a mile," recalled Clinkenbeard, "and lay without fire all night. If the Indians came on the camp, we were to attack them on their rear."

But the Indians did not return. On August 9, the Kentuckians burned hundreds of acres of cornfields at Peckuwe, and still more at Lagonda, a small village at modern Springfield. On August 10, they marched south.

Local historian Bill Smith is standing beneath a section of the cliffs that blocked Logan's advance. (Author's photograph)

When Clark reached the Falls on August 22, he dispatched a report to Jefferson. If Logan's regiment had not been "rendered useless for some time by an uncommon chain of rocks that they could not pass," the Kentucky commander wrote, he would have inflicted "a decisive stroke to the Indians." But even so, he reported, "The enemy were totally routed."

He had won with an army that few commanders could have led to victory. His fiercely independent men were not accustomed to taking orders from anyone. But they had obeyed his. "Nothing could excel this little army," he wrote proudly to Jefferson, "in bravery and implicit obedience to orders."

He had also won without incurring the massive casualties he had feared. He had anticipated every stratagem of the Indians. Only 30 Kentuckians had died or been mortally wounded at the battle.

The Indians had suffered casualties at least as large. But the gravest damage was to their cornfields. The day Clark wrote to Jefferson, McKee dispatched a desperate letter to de Peyster. Unless the British commander immediately sent the Shawnees food and ammunition from Detroit, McKee wrote, "they must perish."

Clark did not, however, report to the Virginia governor all that had happened. When he had returned to the Falls from Fort Jefferson, he had found awaiting him a petition signed by 672 settlers. It had called for a Kentucky declaration of independence. As he had marched back from Peckuwe, his men had asked him to become Kentucky's leader. They began, he wrote to his father on August 23, "soliciting me to head them as their Governor General." He refused, Clark added, "my duty obliging me to suppress all such proceedings."

The Kentuckians, Clark thought, could not see. They and their children would never have a secure future in a small, weak bastion of freedom on the frontier. But they would have one in a powerful United States that extended to the Great Lakes and the Mississippi. To create that, they must capture Detroit.

Clark's victory had calmed the panic that had followed the fall of Ruddell's and Martin's stations. But the threat that the settlers would abandon Kentucky remained. "A great number of those who had been considered permanent settlers in the country," Bradford remembered, "removed to the old settled country in the autumn of the year 1780."

On October 1, Clark joined the departing settlers. Men like McIntosh and Brodhead, he thought, would never take Detroit, but he could. Back across the mountains he would get what he would need. Washington must provide regulars and artillery, and Jefferson militiamen and supplies. Then, with Kentuckians that Floyd, Linn, Harrod, and Logan would raise, he would end at last the war on the Ohio River frontier.

This 1996 bust of Clark by Ann S. Allen is at Locust Grove, the house of his sister Lucy Clark Croghan, where Clark died in 1818. (Courtesy of Historic Locust Grove, Louisville, Kentucky)

GEORGE ROGERS CLARK
1752 — 1818
founder of Louisville
Conqueror of the Northwest Territory
Trails End ...
Locust Grove
dedicated 1986

AFTERMATH

THE END OF THE REVOLUTIONARY WAR

When Clark reached Richmond, the new Virginia capital, he found growing alarm. Eight days after Peckuwe, Cornwallis had destroyed a 3,700-man American army at the August 16, 1780 Battle of Camden. He had then dispatched Major Patrick Ferguson west to organize a loyalist army. Militiamen led by Shelby and the famous Tennessee commander John Sevier had annihilated Ferguson's 1,100 loyalists at the October 7, 1780 Battle of King's Mountain, killing or capturing them all. But Cornwallis had sent Lieutenant-Colonel Banastre Tarleton with regulars to rally the loyalists. The fighting was spreading ever further north, and Morgan had come out of retirement to defend Virginia.

Jefferson nonetheless responded favorably to his proposal, and Washington agreed. As "brigadier general of the forces to be embodied on an expedition west of the Ohio," Clark would have Gibson's 13th Virginia artillery from Fort Pitt, and two Virginia militia regiments. He would raise hundreds of Virginia and Pennsylvania recruits on the upper Ohio, and then join the Kentuckians. With Gibson as his second in command, he would lead a 3,000-man army against Detroit.

Soon after Clark left for Pittsburgh, news recalled him to Richmond. Encouraged by Cornwallis' success, the British had dispatched a second army to Virginia. Led by British Brigadier-General Benedict Arnold, who four months before had been an American major-general, 1,600 men had landed on the James River on January 3, 1781. They had then burned Richmond and withdrawn to a base further downriver.

What followed offered a glimpse of the career Clark might have had if he had followed Cresap, Morgan, and Crawford across the mountains. When he reached the ruined Virginia capital, Jefferson gave him command of a hastily collected force of 240 local militiamen. Word then arrived that the able Lieutenant-Colonel John Graves Simcoe was marching back up

After King's Mountain, Shelby and Sevier turned their attention to the Cherokees, whose lands were ravaged in 1781, 1782, and 1783 campaigns. Shelby kept this captured British musket as a souvenir of King's Mountain. (Kentucky Historical Society, 1939.224)

the James River. Simcoe, who had learned that Jefferson was in Richmond, was advancing quickly in an attempt to capture him.

On January 10, Simcoe's formidable force of 420 loyalist rangers and Hessian irregulars found at Cabin Point the reception that Clark had prepared. Forty of Clark's militiamen fired on the British and fled. Simcoe's pursuing men then rushed into an ambush by Clark's other 200 Virginians. At a cost of four wounded, Clark's militiamen killed 17, wounded 13, and ended Simcoe's operation.

The threat to Virginia then briefly eased. Continental Army regiments arrived to defend Richmond, and Morgan destroyed Tarleton's army at the January 17, 1781 Battle of Cowpens. On January 22, Clark left for Pittsburgh with a letter from Washington to Brodhead. "I do not think," the Continental Army commander had written, "the charge of the enterprise could have been committed to better hands than Col. Clark."

After White Eyes' death, Killbuck had been able to keep the Delawares neutral. But Captain Pipe, still angry at the killing of his relatives, finally persuaded most of the nation's chiefs to join the British. As Clark was riding toward Pittsburgh, they drove Killbuck and his supporters from the principal Delaware town, Coshocton.

The Kentuckian received a cold reception at Fort Pitt. Livid that Clark had been given the command, Brodhead refused to detach Gibson's regiment. He instead led 300 men into Ohio to support Killbuck. On April 20, Brodhead's men and Killbuck's 30 warriors attacked Coshocton, where they killed 20 Delaware warriors. The next day, Killbuck's men defeated another force of 40 Delawares across the Tuscarawas River.

As Brodhead and Killbuck were returning to Pittsburgh, welcome reinforcements arrived in Detroit. Alarmed at news of Clark's planned campaign, the British had dispatched to oppose him the celebrated Mohawk chief Joseph Brant. With Brant had come Mohawk warriors and two

After the war, Simcoe would become the first Lieutenant-Governor of Upper Canada, now Ontario. This 1903 Walter Seymour Allward statue of Simcoe stands in Toronto's Queen's Park. (Toronto Public Library; public domain)

At Cowpens, one of the tactical masterpieces of 18th-century warfare, Morgan lured Tarleton's 1,150-man army into a double envelopment from which Tarleton and about 40 dragoons alone escaped. The photograph shows the Cowpens battlefield today. (National Park Service; public domain)

Joseph Brant, Freemason and translator of the Gospel of St Mark into Mohawk, had dazzled his hosts on a 1775 visit to London. "I will bow to no man, Sir," he had told King George III, "but it would be an honor to shake your hand." His celebrity produced a demand for images of the colorful Mohawk chief. This 1779 J. R. Smith engraving was made from a 1776 portrait by George Romney. (Library and Archives Canada, Acc. No. 1970-188-2383 W.H. Coverdale Collection of Canadiana)

companies of Butler's Rangers, led by captains William Caldwell and Andrew Bradt.

As Clark recruited on the upper Ohio frontier, good news arrived from Floyd. Clark would have 1,200 Kentuckians, and hunters were amassing a vast store of salted buffalo meat to feed them. But the news from across the Appalachians was discouraging. He would have no militiamen from Virginia. The day before the Battle of Coshocton, Cornwallis had defeated another American army at the April 19 Battle of Guilford Courthouse. Now he was marching toward Virginia to join Arnold. Morgan was battling loyalists in the Virginia counties from which Jefferson had planned to send Clark regiments.

The Kentuckian also had trouble finding men on the upper Ohio. The local Pennsylvania leaders, an outraged Colonel John Neville wrote to Clark, "did everything in their power to prevent your campaign." And he could find little food for the Virginians who enlisted.

Few upper Ohio merchants were willing to sell Clark supplies. It now was the same everywhere on the frontier. Three months after Peckuwe, Fort Jefferson had survived an attack by 200 British rangers and Indians. But by 1781, its commandant could no longer find food for his garrison. On June 8, the American stronghold was abandoned.

Clark finally persuaded Brodhead to detach a 30-man artillery company, and succeeded in recruiting 370 Virginians. Jefferson, moreover, persuaded the President of Pennsylvania to provide Colonel Archibald Lochry and 107 Pennsylvania horsemen.

By the end of July, he could wait no longer. His hungry recruits were deserting faster than new men could be found. After waiting five days for Lochry's Pennsylvanians, Clark finally led his artillerymen and recruits down the Ohio on August 7. Two days later, Lochry's men followed.

As the two small American flotillas went down the river on August 20, unwelcome visitors arrived at Gnadenhütten, where the Christian Delaware had just begun harvesting their corn. Elliott, Captain Pipe, and Half King announced that the Christian Delaware were warning the American settlers of coming raids. They now would march immediately to the Sandusky River, where they would live under close supervision at Captives' Town.

As the Christian Delaware left their unharvested corn, Brant, Girty, and 200 warriors were nearing the mouth of the Miami River, where McKee and another 400 were to join them and await for Clark's advance. When Lochry's boats passed the mouth of the Miami, Brant's and Girty's men followed them downstream.

On August 24, Lochry halted at the mouth of Laughery Creek, at present Aurora, IN, so that the Pennsylvanians' horses could graze. Lochry's defeat ended quickly. Without suffering any casualties, Brant's and Girty's warriors killed Lochry and 37 of his scattered men, and took the others captive.

Two days later, Clark reached the Falls, where his principal Kentucky commanders were waiting. Todd, who had returned from Cahokia, was among them, but a man that Clark had relied on was not. Linn had been killed by Indian raiders on March 15.

Because of the raiding, they told Clark, few Kentuckians were willing to march to Detroit. There also would be little food. Floyd's hunters had accumulated at Painted Stone Station 50 tons of buffalo meat, but raiders had killed the men bringing salt to preserve it.

As Clark and his officers debated whether to proceed with the campaign, their alarm at Lochry's failure to arrive grew. On September 6, scouts returned to report his fate. It was the end. Clark was forced to cancel the campaign. In it, the devastated commander later wrote, "my very soul was wrapped."

On September 9, McKee's warriors finally joined Brant's and Girty's. But Brant and Girty quarreled. After nearly killing Girty with his sword, Brant left with most of the Indians. McKee then led the remaining 200 into Kentucky to attack Painted Stone Station.

On September 13, McKee's warriors overtook the fleeing Painted Stone Station settlers 5 miles northwest of present Shelbyville, killing 15 at the Long Run Massacre. When Floyd, Wells, and 25 others reached the site on September 14 to retrieve the bodies, they were ambushed at Floyd's Defeat. Floyd, Wells and seven others, all wounded, alone survived.

At the fort at the Falls, now renamed Fort Nelson, a depressed Clark watched the end of the year approach. But on a dark November day, news arrived so glorious that it relieved even Clark's gloom. Trapped at Yorktown, Cornwallis had on October 19 surrendered his and Arnold's armies, more than 9,000 men in all.

Excited again, Clark proposed a 1782 campaign against Detroit to Benjamin Harrison, Virginia's new governor. The fighting, Harrison

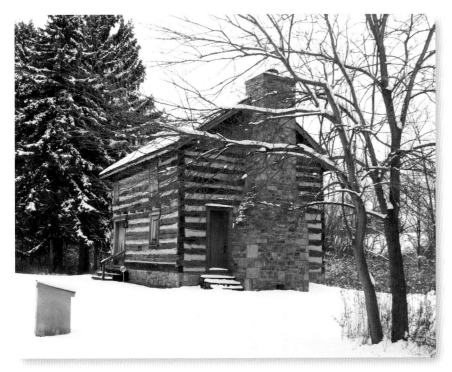

In 2002, Lochry's blockhouse was found beneath the clapboard siding and asphalt shingles of an abandoned house in Latrobe, PA. Now restored, the structure is preserved near its original site. (Courtesy of Winnie Palmer Nature Reserve at Saint Vincent College)

responded on December 20, now was over. John Adams, Benjamin Franklin, and John Jay were in Paris negotiating a peace treaty. The British had ordered the Indians to cease operations against the settlers. If there was a continuing need for defense, Clark should build new forts at the points where Indian trails crossed the Ohio River.

As snow covered the Ohio frontier, the starving Christian Delaware at Captives' Town despaired. "Many times," remembered Susan Zeisberger, the wife of the captives' minister, "I spent eight days in succession without food of my own." The Delaware and Wyandot chiefs finally agreed to allow 100 of the captives to return briefly to their abandoned fields to search for food.

When Williamson's men voted 143 to 18 to kill the Indians at Gnadenhütten, the dissenters removed themselves to a site beyond the town. After the massacre, one remembered, a crying Wallace joined them. "You know I couldn't help it," he said between sobs. This monument in Gnadenhütten, OH, is at the site of the massacre. (Author's photograph)

The new year then revealed whether the fighting was over. On February 10, 1782, Robert Wallace returned to his cabin 15 miles northwest of Pittsburgh to find it burned and his wife and three children missing. A few days later, raiders captured John Carpenter. Two of his captors, Carpenter reported after escaping, had said that they were Christian Delaware.

On March 1, Colonel David Williamson and 160 militiamen marched to Gnadenhütten. There Wallace saw among the starving Indians scouring the fields for food a woman wearing his wife's dress. She had bought the blood-stained garment from a Wyandot, she said. But she was not believed. On March 8, Williamson's men killed 96 Christian Delaware at the Gnadenhütten Massacre.

By then, raiders were killing again in Kentucky. Captain James Estill and 25 men pursued 25 raiders to near what is now Mt Sterling, KY. On March 22, the pursued ambushed their pursuers. At Estill's Defeat, they killed Estill and six others, and wounded most of the rest. By the end of March, they had killed 40 more Kentuckians.

Many of the upper Ohio settlers were outraged at the killing of the Christian Delaware, but others thought that any Indian should be killed on sight. A worried Gibson sent guards to protect Killbuck's Delawares, who were camped within sight of Fort Pitt. But two days after Estill's defeat, settlers overpowered the guards, and killed at the Killbuck Island Massacre Brady's friend Nanowland and several other loyal American allies.

About to be captured, Crawford shattered his sword beside what would be named Broken Sword Creek. These fragments are displayed at the Wyandot County Museum in Upper Sandusky, OH. (Courtesy of the Wyandot County Historical Society, Upper Sandusky, OH)

In response to settlers' pleas, Crawford agreed to lead 500 upper Ohio militiamen against the Indian towns on the Sandusky River. But they found waiting Caldwell, McKee, Elliott, Girty, Captain Pipe, and 700 warriors and British rangers. Surrounded for two days at the June 4–5 Battle of Upper Sandusky, the Americans finally broke through their attackers. Overtaken, they drove off their pursuers at the June 6 Battle of the Olentangy. Seventy, however, never recrossed the Ohio. Crawford was captured and tortured to death.

A month later, the Seneca chief Guyasuta led a force of 160 Mingos, Senecas, and British rangers down the Allegheny River. On July 13, they burned Hannastown and several nearby settlements, killing 20 settlers, and capturing 20 more.

It then again was the turn of Kentucky. On August 15–16, 350 warriors and British rangers, led by Caldwell, McKee, Girty, and Blue Jacket, besieged Bryan's Station. A hundred and eighty-two Kentuckians led by Todd, and another 200 led by Logan, rushed to relieve the fort. When Todd's men arrived, the besiegers withdrew.

After pursuing the Indians and rangers to Blue Licks on the Licking River, most of Todd's men wanted to wait for Logan's, but McGary was impatient. "Them that ain't cowards," he shouted on August 19, "follow me." And they did. At the Battle of Blue Licks, Todd, Bulger, and 70 others fell, and McMurtry and ten others were captured.

As the Americans reeled from the blows, the assault continued in September. In Kentucky, 150 Indians captured Kincheloe Station on September 1, killing 13. On the upper Ohio, 350 Indians and rangers, led by Captain Andrew Bradt, besieged Fort Henry from September 11 to 13.

Through it all, Clark had sat in his cabin at the Falls. No militiamen had appeared to build the forts Harrison had ordered. And no one would sell food or supplies for promises of future payment. The food his Illinois Regiment men ate, Clark paid for with his own dwindling funds.

Stung by Blue Licks, the Kentuckians again asked Clark to lead a campaign against the Shawnees. When he received no response to a request for approval by Harrison, he finally agreed. When no one would provide the 70,000lb of flour the Kentuckians would eat, he sold 3,500 acres of his land to obtain it.

Caldwell, a Pennsylvania loyalist, would prove a formidable leader in western battles. After the war, he would lead his men, by then called Caldwell's Rangers, against the Americans at Fallen Timbers, and later at Thames. These Caldwell's Rangers re-enactors are refighting Blue Licks at Blue Licks Battlefield State Resort Park. Some are wearing the black leather caps and green coats issued to Butler's Rangers in 1777. (Graphic Enterprises)

The 1782 siege of Fort Henry would be remembered for the daring run of 17-year-old Betty Zane to and from a nearby cabin for powder needed by the defenders. This 1903 Louis F. Grant engraving, which depicts the exploit, illustrated *Betty Zane*, a biography written by the novelist Zane Grey, her great-grandnephew. (Author's collection)

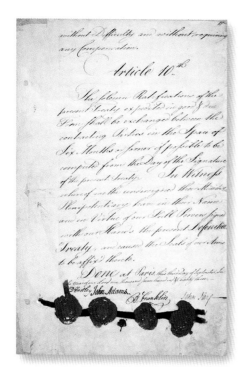

The 1782 Treaty of Paris was contingent on peace between Britain and France. After the contingency was fulfilled, a final version was signed on September 3, 1783. Its last page has the signatures of Hartley, Adams, Franklin, and Jay. (US National Archives)

On November 1, Clark led 1,050 Kentuckians across the Ohio in the last American operation of the Revolutionary War. On November 10, his men destroyed Chalawgatha, which had been rebuilt on the Miami River at modern Troy. The following day, they destroyed rebuilt Peckuwe, at what is now Piqua. Clark then sent Logan and 150 horsemen to burn Loramie's Trading Post.

A defiant Clark remained for four days, daring the Indians to attack. Let them come, he announced, under any commander, in any number – but no Indians came. The Kentuckians, who had lost one dead and one wounded, recrossed the Ohio on November 18. The following day, their commander celebrated his 30th birthday.

Thousands had died on the Ohio frontier during the war. In Kentucky alone, 860 militiamen had fallen. Fewer than 40, however, had died in Clark's campaigns. And of all the war's western operations, time would reveal, only his had mattered.

Clark had been denied an opportunity to take Detroit, but he had done enough. Two months after Peckuwe, Congress had given instructions to Adams, Franklin, and Jay. Because of Clark's capture of Kaskaskia, Cahokia, and Vincennes, they were to demand that Britain recognize as the western American border the Great Lakes and the Mississippi.

Eleven days after Clark's birthday, the three American negotiators made a momentous visit to 56 Rue Jacob in Paris, where the British diplomat David Hartley lived. On September 30, 1782, they signed a treaty ending the Revolutionary War. In the Treaty of Paris, Britain agreed to surrender Detroit, and to recognize as American territory what would become the states of Kentucky, Ohio, Indiana, Illinois, Michigan, and Wisconsin.

AFTER THE REVOLUTIONARY WAR

The war, however, did not end in American parades and celebrations. It ended in chaos, fear, and anger. Everywhere Americans demanded payment for military service, for supplies they had provided, for money they had lent. And everywhere there were American governments and men who could not pay.

On the Ohio River frontier, moreover, there was not even peace. Any doubt disappeared on April 8, 1783, when Indian raiders killed Floyd. Despite the Treaty of Paris, the British refused to surrender Detroit. Indian raiders would kill about three Kentuckians a week for the next ten years.

They found more targets every year. Five thousand Revolutionary War officers and soldiers received warrants for land in Kentucky. Tens of thousands of other immigrants joined them. Soon the original Kentucky settlers were but a small fraction of the population.

As new faces appeared almost daily in Kentucky, Clark received a December 4, 1783 letter from Jefferson. A daring party of frontiersmen, Jefferson thought, now should explore what lay in "the country from the Mississippi to California." "How would you like to lead such a party?" he asked. Clark sadly declined. "Your proposition," Clark replied, "would be extremely agreeable to me could I afford it."

As he had fought Black Fish's raiders in 1777, Clark had pondered in the western wilderness the significance of the birth of the United States. He had chosen to fight for its future. "The interest and welfare of the public," he had resolved, was to be "my only concern until the fate of the continent could be known." He could afford such patriotism, Clark had thought. After the war, his land holdings would make him one of Kentucky's richest men.

But when his Illinois Regiment had disbanded in 1783, he had found himself impoverished. He had nothing, Clark wrote, "except what the state owes me." And the prospects of payment were dim. Virginia's leaders wanted to avoid paying any debts that could be questioned. And some, like Harrison, were eager to question the huge amounts owed for Clark's operations in the West.

Clark had fought the British and Indians, but his most dangerous enemies had proved to be American. "That you have enemies, you must not doubt," Jefferson had written to warn him after his 1782 campaign. "When you enterprised deeds which will hand down your name with honor to future times, you made yourself a mark for malice and envy to shoot at."

Then came horrifying news. When Arnold's soldiers had burned Richmond, Clark was told, they had destroyed the expense records he had sent to Virginia. Without them, exactly what was owed could never be determined. He and his suppliers would never be paid.

The catastrophe left Clark worse than penniless. He lost his honor along with his money and land. Vigo and others who had trusted him were ruined. "Everything I have is going to be sold for some debt that I contracted for part of the goods you got from me," wrote a Pittsburgh merchant. And men like the owner of the corn he had requisitioned to save the Peckuwe campaign could complain that they had been "robbed by a thief."

If Virginia would not pay, many of Clark's suppliers claimed, then he must. Their suits left him indebted for a sum no American could pay. Any property he would ever own, his creditors would seize.

This snow-covered 1936 John Angel statue at George Rogers Clark National Historical Park depicts Vigo, who lost his fortune aiding Clark. (National Park Service)

The betrayed Kentuckian lost Teresa too. Her uncle, one of Clark's nieces remembered, "thought it not honorable for him to marry a lady educated as she was and accustomed to all the luxuries of wealth without having any means of supporting her."

His achievements, moreover, seemed every day less significant. The United States, most thought, had been just an alliance of the 13 states to prosecute the war. Its distant border on the Great Lakes and Mississippi was just an unimportant line on a map.

It was enough to drive a man to drink – and Clark was driven. Only the arrival in Kentucky of his extended family relieved his despair. Led by his elder brother Jonathan, a brigadier-general in Washington's army, Clark's relatives began creating in 1784 a private world in which he could find solace. There Clark began teaching his 14-year-old brother William the skills of an Ohio River frontiersman.

Wilkinson conducted his operation from his new settlement, Frankfort, which would become Kentucky's capital. Beneath the clapboard siding of this house, razed in 1870, was the log house Wilkinson built in Frankfort in 1786. (Author's collection)

In 1784, Virginia ended its interest in the West by transferring its territory beyond the Ohio River to the United States. Spain then crippled the Kentucky economy by closing the Mississippi River to American traffic. Two parties debated the path that Kentucky should follow. Shelby, who had returned in 1783, led one, which called for Kentucky to join the United States as a new state. James Wilkinson, who arrived in 1784, led the other. It argued that Kentucky should become an independent country allied with Spain.

As the Kentuckians argued, Clark performed a last service for the United States. After assuming authority over the territory transferred by Virginia, Congress asked Clark to serve as a commissioner in peace negotiations with the Ohio Indians. Many prominent chiefs, including Buckongahelas, Captain Pipe, and Half King, agreed to the January 31, 1786 Treaty of Fort Finney. But the raiding continued.

On August 2, 1786, the militia officers of Kentucky petitioned Clark to lead a campaign against the Miami towns on the Wabash, from which warriors were threatening Vincennes. Without any aid from Virginia, they promised, they would raise 2,500 men and provide all the supplies he would need. Clark reluctantly agreed.

Clark's reappearance as a prominent figure alarmed Wilkinson, who hoped to rule an independent Kentucky. He had used his skills as a conspirator, defamer, and saboteur to rise to the rank of brigadier-general in the Continental Army. Now he used them in a covert campaign against his dangerous rival.

Some of Wilkinson's agents worked in Kentucky, discouraging enlistment or the provision of supplies. Others labored beyond the mountains, warning officials of the United States and Virginia that, under the guise of raising an army to fight Indians, Clark was assembling a force to conquer Spanish Louisiana.

By the time they had done their noxious work, only 950 men had joined the Kentucky army, 550 had deserted for lack of food, and Clark had canceled the campaign. Logan, who had returned to Kentucky to find more men for the campaign, had led 800 Kentuckians into Ohio, where they had burned seven Mad River villages. The governor of Virginia had called for Clark's arrest, and the United States had apologized to Spain for Clark's imagined plan to seize Louisiana.

A baffled and disgusted Clark then tried to restore his fortune. He planned new settlements beyond the Ohio and the Mississippi. But his schemes failed.

In 1788, order began to appear in the chaos that had followed the Revolutionary War. The states agreed to the new US Constitution, and Washington assumed office as the first US President. In 1791, he sent General Arthur St Clair's new US Army to suppress the Indians. Clark watched Oldham lead 260 militiamen off to fight with St Clair, and Wells return from Wabash with the few who survived.

In 1792, when Kentucky entered the union, the American economy at last began to recover. A hopeful Jonathan Clark asked Congress and the Virginia legislature to make special appropriations to compensate Clark for his loss. To the horror of Jefferson and many others, they refused.

The bitter Kentuckian then made a last effort to escape from his prison of debt. When the new French revolutionary government decided to seize Spanish Louisiana in 1793, Clark offered his services. Commissioned a French major-general, he began recruiting in Kentucky an army to capture St Louis and New Orleans. Logan responded with enthusiasm. Shelby, Kentucky's first governor, offered covert support. But Washington ordered Anthony Wayne, who had created a new US Army to replace St Clair's, to oppose any advance by Clark's force. The Kentuckian then disbanded his men.

Clark lived to see Wayne defeat the Indians at Fallen Timbers in 1794, and enter Detroit in triumph in 1796; and on to see the United States purchase the Louisiana Territory in 1803. By then, Logan, Harrod, and many others who had fought with him were dead. Boone had left Kentucky for Upper Louisiana, which would soon become the American Missouri Territory. Kenton had moved to the new state of Ohio, and Clark and his younger brother William were living in a small cabin in what is now Clarksville, IN.

There William Clark received a letter from Meriwether Lewis, a friend he had made while serving as one of Wayne's captains. It offered an opportunity he welcomed. On October 14, 1803, Lewis arrived at the Clark brothers' cabin, where he and William Clark began planning the exploring expedition the two would lead. Twelve days later, the elder Clark watched them depart on the journey to the Pacific he had foregone 20 years before.

Clark lived another 15 years. Although he seldom communicated with anyone but relatives and close friends, he sometimes received correspondence. "We are both now grown old," Jefferson wrote to him on December 19, 1807, "but in all times and places, I shall wish you every happiness and salute you with great friendship and esteem." "The meritorious services of the best patriots of those days," wrote Vigo on July 15, 1811, "were too easily forgotten by my adopted country with ingratitude."

Four months after Vigo wrote his letter, Clark saw Wells and Floyd's son George Rogers Clark Floyd return from Tippecanoe, where Benjamin Harrison's son William Henry had led them to victory. Two years later, he learned that his sister Lucy's son George Croghan had become a national hero for his defense of Fort Stephenson during the War of 1812. Soon after came word of the younger Harrison's victory at Thames, which ended the Ohio Indian wars.

Of the great commanders in those wars, Clark most resembled the 12-year-old boy who had wanted to fight him at Peckuwe. Both emerged from obscurity, astonished their contemporaries for five years, and then passed from view. Both had rare strategic vision, and both had a gift for the theatrical that added glowing color to their legends.

When Meriwether Lewis arrived at the Clark brothers' cabin, he gave this compass to William Clark, who carried it on the Lewis and Clark expedition. (Division of Political History, National Museum of American History, Smithsonian Institution)

After losing a leg in an accident, Clark spent his last nine years in this room at Locust Grove. (Photograph by John Nation; courtesy of Historic Locust Grove, Louisville, Kentucky)

Tecumseh's vision was never fulfilled, but his legend ended in a heroic death at Thames. Clark lived to see his realized, but died a man who had seen too much. "Come on my brave boys, St Vin," he said at the end in 1818.

After Clark's death, clerks in Richmond discovered that his expense records had not been destroyed, but only misplaced. For decades, Virginia determined what had been owed to Clark and his suppliers, and paid to their heirs the amounts due. As Clark's nephews and nieces received their payments, a quarter of the American population occupied the territory he had battled to win for their nation. By 1875, when Vigo's descendants received their last payment, the monuments had begun to appear.

Their inscriptions would record Clark's achievements, but none would match in eloquence the wordless judgment of a man who had fought at Peckuwe. US Army Ensign Ebenezer Denny saw him arrive at the Fort Finney peace council. "Buckongahelas," Denny wrote in his journal on January 21, 1786, "is esteemed one of the greatest warriors now among the Indians. After he had seated himself, he discovered General Clark, and knowing him to be a great warrior, rose and saluted him very significantly. Instead of taking hold of each other's hands, they gripped nearly at the shoulder, and shook the left hands underneath the right arms."

The George Rogers Clark Memorial at George Rogers Clark National Historical Park in Vincennes, IN, at sunset on Christmas Eve. (National Park Service)

THE BATTLEFIELD TODAY

The sites of Chalawgatha and Peckuwe can be visited today. Oldtown Reserve, a park on US Route 28 about 3 miles north of Xenia, OH, occupies the southeasternmost portion of Chalawgatha. The site of Peckuwe is now George Rogers Clark Park at 930 South Tecumseh Road near Springfield, OH. The nearby Davidson Interpretative Center has exhibits on the battle.

The sites of many events before Clark's campaign also can be seen. Boonesborough and Harrodsburg have been reconstructed at Fort Boonesborough State Park near Richmond, KY, and Old Fort Harrod State Park in Harrodsburg, KY. The Cumberland Gap is now Cumberland Gap National Park near Middlesboro, KY. Joseph Martin's Station has been reconstructed at Wilderness Road State Park near Middlesboro, KY. Fort Pitt is now the Fort Pitt Museum in Point State Park in Pittsburgh. Fort Randolph has been reconstructed in Krodel Park in Point Pleasant, West VA. The Kaskaskia Bell State Historic Site in Kaskaskia, IL, preserves the bell rung there when Clark's army arrived. The house of a French settler in Cahokia survives at Cahokia Courthouse State Historic Site in Illinois. The site of Fort Sackville is now George Rogers Clark National Historical Park in Vincennes, IN.

The battlefield today.
(Author's map)

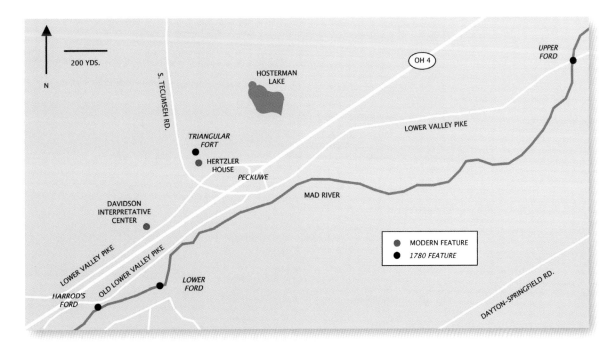

Many other sites referred to in the book also can be visited. Those include reconstructed Schoenbrunn Village in New Philadelphia, OH; Gnadenhutten Museum and Park in Gnadenhutten, OH, Fort Laurens in Bolivar, OH; reconstructed Prickett's Fort in Fairmont, West VA; Blue Licks Battlefield State Resort Park near Carlisle, KY; Historic Hanna's Town near Greensburg, PA; and reconstructed Fort Michilimackinac, in Mackinaw City, MI.

Many other sites are associated with figures in the book. A reproduction of George Rogers and William Clark's cabin is on its original site at Falls of the Ohio State Park in Clarksville, IN. Locust Grove, where Clark died, survives as Historic Locust Grove in Louisville. Daniel Boone was born at the Daniel Boone Homestead in Birdsboro, PA, and died at the Historic Daniel Boone Home in Defiance, MO. Simon Kenton is celebrated at Historic Washington in Maysville, KY, where many 18th-century cabins survive at their original sites. William and Esther Whitley's house survives at the William Whitley House State Historic Site in Stanford, KY. Robert Patterson's cabin in Lexington is preserved on the grounds of Transylvania University. His 1816 house in Dayton, OH, survives as the Patterson Homestead.

FURTHER READING

Bakeless, John, *Background to Glory: The Life of George Rogers Clark* (1957)

Barker, Gerry, *Some Thoughts on Scouts and Spies* (2010)

Carstens, Kenneth C. and Nancy (eds.), *The Life of George Rogers Clark, 1752–1818: Triumphs and Tragedies* (2004)

Clark, Thomas D. (ed.), *Voice of the Frontier: John Bradford's Notes on Kentucky* (1993)

De Haas, Wills, *History of the Early Settlement and Indian Wars of Western Virginia* (1851)

Doddridge, Joseph, *Notes on the Settlement and Indian Wars of the Western Parts of Virginia and Pennsylvania from 1763 to 1783* (1912)

English, William H., *Conquest of the Country Northwest of the River Ohio, 1778–1783* (1895)

Hall, Henry, "Bowman's Campaign – 1779," *Ohio Archaeological and Historical Society Quarterly*, v. 22, pp.515–19 (Columbus, OH, 1913)

Hammon, Neal O. and Taylor, Richard, *Virginia's Western War, 1775–1786* (2002)

Harding, Margery H., *George Rogers Clark and his Men: Military Records, 1778–1784* (1981)

Harrison, Lowell H., *George Rogers Clark and the War in the West* (2014)

Hintzen, William, *The Border Wars of the Upper Ohio Valley (1769–1794)* (1999)

Hoffman, Phillip W., *Simon Girty: Turncoat Hero* (2008)

Howard, James H., *Shawnee! The Ceremonialism of a Native American Tribe and its Cultural Background* (1981)

Kellogg, Louise P., *Frontier Advance on the Upper Ohio, 1778–1779* (1916)

——, *Frontier Retreat on the Upper Ohio, 1779–1781* (1917)

Kramb, Edwin A., *Buckeye Battlefields* (1999)

McConnell, Michael N., *A Country Between: The Upper Ohio Valley and its Peoples, 1724–1774* (1992)

Nester, William R., *George Rogers Clark: I Glory in War* (2012)

Olmstead, Earl P., *Blackcoats Among the Delaware: David Zeisberger on the Ohio Frontier* (1991)

Pieper, Thomas I. and Gladney, James B., *Fort Laurens, 1778–1779* (1976)

Sipe, C. Hale, *The Indian Wars of Pennsylvania* (1929)

Sugden, John, *Blue Jacket: Warrior of the Shawnees* (2000)

Tanner, Helen H., *Atlas of Great Lakes Indian History* (1987)

Thwaites, Reuben G. and Kellogg, Louise P., *Frontier Defense on the Upper Ohio, 1777–1778* (1912)

West, J. Martin, "Clark's 1780 Peckuwe Campaign," in Kenneth C. Carstens and Nancy Carstens (eds.), *The Life of George Rogers Clark, 1752–1818: Triumphs and Tragedies* (2004), pp.176–97

West, J. Martin, *Clark's Shawnee Campaign of 1780: Contemporary Accounts* (1975)

Winkler, John F., *Point Pleasant 1774, Preface to the American Revolution* (Osprey Campaign Series No. 273, 2014)

INDEX